A PHOTO-LOCATION AND HILL WALKING GUIDEBOOK

PHOTOGRAPHING
THE SNOWDONIA MOUNTAINS

FOREWORD BY SIR CHRIS BONINGTON

NICK LIVESEY

Project managed and edited by Mick Ryan – fotoVUE Ltd.

fotoVUE Mountain Series design by Ryder Design and fotoVUE Ltd.

Layout and production by Ryder Design – *www.ryderdesign.studio*

Additional graphics by Mick Ryan.

All maps within this publication were produced by Don Williams of Bute Cartographics.
Maps contain Ordnance Survey data © Crown copyright and database right 2018.

A CIP catalogue record for this book is available from the British Library.

ISBN 978-0-9929051-9-4
10 9 8 7 6 5 4 3 2 1

The author, publisher and others involved in the design and publication of this guide book accept no responsibility for any loss or damage users may suffer as a result of using this book. Users of this book are responsible for their own safety and use the information herein at their own risk. Users should always be aware of weather forecasts, conditions, time of day and their own ability before venturing out.

Front cover: *Dan Aspel on Castell y Gwynt on a March afternoon. Four Shot stitched panorama. Canon 6D, 24 - 70 at 24mm, ISO 100, 1/125 sec at f/11, 0.9 graduated filter, tripod.* **Rear cover left**: *Moel Siabod and the Snowdon Range from Pen y Geuallt on an August evening. Six shot stitched panorama. Canon 7D, 17-40mm at 17mm, ISO 100, 1/5 sec at f/11, 0.9 graduated filter, tripod.* **Rear cover centre**: *High water in the Afon Llugwy rushing beneath Pont Cyfyng. Canon 6D, 17-40mm at 17mm, ISO 100, 1 sec at f/8, ND filter, tripod.* **Rear cover right**: *Tryfan from Carnedd y Filiast, March afternoon. Canon 7D, 17-40mm at 33mm, ISO 100, 1/160 sec at f/11.*

Printed and bound in Europe by Latitude Press Ltd.

Only a hill: earth set a little higher
Above the face of the earth: a larger view
Of little fields and roads: a little nigher
To clouds, and silence: what is that to you?
Only a hill: but all of life to me,
Up there, between the sunset and the sea.

GEOFFREY WINTHROP YOUNG

Contents

THE WALKS

ROADSIDE LOCATIONS & SHORT WALKS

Jamie Rooke and the Snowdon Massif from Bwlch y Marchlyn.
Canon 6D, 24-70mm at 47mm, ISO 100, 1/100 sec at f/11, 0.9 graduated filter

***Overleaf**: Karl Page enjoying a December temperature inversion on Glyder Fach.*
Canon 6D, 24-70mm at 29mm, ISO 100, 1/400 sec at f/11, 0.9 graduated filter.

Acknowledgements

I am indebted to so many people and would hate not to give mention to anyone who has helped me during the writing of this book. To mention you all, however, would require more space than I have available to me so if I don't thank you here then I certainly will in person.

Firstly, I would like to dedicate this book to Lucie Sedlarova who, through much soul-searching, sent me on my way to find my true calling, a life in the mountains. I hope the words and pictures within these pages bring back fond memories of the times we shared on the ridges, crags and summits (not forgetting the chip shops) of Snowdonia.

Dorina, Gabriela and Paul earn my sincere gratitude for giving me a start in Wales and acting as a surrogate family (along with the rest of Team Siabod). How could you have known what you were letting yourselves in for? John Rowell and Marion Waine have, as my partners in the *Soul of Snowdonia Gallery* been loyal friends and endured my wayward nature from day one of our friendship. Wear your halos with pride. Jamie Griggs and Barry Williams, you were there at the start of my hill walking 'career' and many years before. I treasure the days we spent together in the hills and all the many other life experiences we've shared along the way.

For inspiration, support and friendship during my time living in Snowdonia my thanks go to Rob Johnson, Paul Poole, Nick Matthews, Greg Knowles, Kevin O'brian, Lara Turner, Caroline Barker, Karl Page, Kris Williams, Andy Woodside, Dan Aspel, Bud Digby Tilton, Susan Forsyth, Greg Whitton, Branwen Mcbride, Phillip Milton, James Hobson, Andrew Yu, Tabitha and Elton Angle-Smith, Rob and Julie Pearson, Steve and Helen Howe, Jock Andrews and Liz Smith.

Helen Iles, Nick and Karl Page on Tryfan, the final peak of the 'Oggie 8' challenge. Sony A6000, 16-50mm at 16mm, ISO 100, 1/80 sec at f/8.

Ethan Walker and Mammut United Kingdom have throughout the writing of this book supported me with some of the best kit known to man. Many thanks for keeping me warm and dry.

The Wainwrights and Edgars of the Tyn y Coed Hotel deserve a special mention for their wonderful hospitality and making sure I've never gone hungry or thirsty in the past five and a half years.

It is a very real thrill to have had the foreword of my book written by a genuine living legend. Your writings, photography and mountaineering exploits have been a huge inspiration to me from the moment I became aware of these great games we play in the mountains. Thank you, Sir Chris.

Don Williams of Bute Cartographics, thank you for your stunning maps to accompany my text and photographs, and all beautifully laid out by Nathan Ryder of Ryder Design, thank you.

Mum, Jemma, Gavin and the brats, I hope this book encourages you to come and visit Snowdonia more often. I really miss you. To my beautiful daughters Hannah and Christina, you are never far from my thoughts.

Last but certainly not least, Mick Ryan of fotoVUE. Working with you has been such a pleasure and I am incredibly grateful that you gave me the opportunity to create something I am very proud of. You're not just my publisher, you are a true friend. Thank you.

***Overleaf**: An incredible November dawn on Crimpiau with Moel Siabod, the Glyderau and the Ogwen Valley beyond. Six shot stitched panorama. Canon 7D, 17-40mm at 17mm, ISO 100, 0.3 sec at f/11, 0.9 graduated filter, tripod*

Foreword by Sir Chris Bonington

The mountains of Snowdonia are at the very roots of my deep passion for climbing and wild mountain spaces. It goes back to the New Year of 1952 when I was just seventeen. My home was in Hampstead, a leafy suburb of North London where I attended the local school. The previous autumn I had glimpsed the Snowdon massif from the Dun Laoghaire/Holyhead Ferry and had been intrigued by the shape of the mountains and the valleys curling into their midst.

I decided to climb Snowdon, and I persuaded one of my school mates to join me. Looking back, it amazes me that my mum, a single parent, and Anton's parents even allowed us to go. We hitchhiked to Capel Curig, stayed in the youth hostel and then set out for Pen y Pass. It was one of the hardest winters for years and Snowdon was plastered in snow and wreathed in cloud. I had a pair of hobnailed army boots and Anton just had his school shoes and macintosh. I had persuaded Mum to cut down my old school raincoat into a jacket. We'd probably have never set out, but there were a couple of guys in the car park with ice axes who looked as if they knew what they were doing, so we just followed them, making our way along the route of the PYG track which was totally concealed by snow. We'd got about halfway across on the flanks of Crib Goch when we were avalanched and in a breathless few seconds swept down several hundred feet toward Glaslyn. My story could so very easily have ended there – but fortunately we weren't swept over any cliffs and ended up on top of the snow, in my case in a state of glorious exhilaration. We turned back and retreated to Pen y Pass, hitching a lift back to the youth hostel in Capel Curig.

The next morning Anton hitchhiked back to London never to venture into the hills again. But I was hooked and stayed on. On returning home I found a family friend who was a climber and he took me on my first climb at Harrison Rocks, a little sandstone outcrop to the south of London, and in the spring holidays I again hitchhiked up to Snowdonia, stayed in youth hostels and found people to climb with.

I was lucky. I found some wonderful mentors but also frequently climbed with people who knew as little as I did. It was a journey of discovery and having the fortune of natural ability I led or shared the lead almost from the beginning. I hitchhiked everywhere, starting by staying in youth hostels then, as I got to know more climbers, I focused on the Llanberis Pass, bivouacking under the boulders below Dinas Mot or in the road menders hut below Dinas Cromlech, and climbing several routes a day, in all weathers, with the enthusiasm of youth. Most of my climbing was in Snowdonia with ventures up to Scotland in the long summer holidays.

My passion was climbing but I couldn't imagine making a living from it. I ended up going to Sandhurst and being commissioned in the Royal Tank Regiment. This took me abroad for the first time as my regiment was stationed in Munster giving me the opportunity of reaching the Alps and plunging into extreme alpinism, until a posting to the newly formed Army Outward Bound School took me to Towyn in North Wales.

Opposite: Chris Bonington age 15 after his first ever climb in 1951.
Photo: *Chris Bonington Picture Library*

That two years posting in the late fifties, taking our students, junior soldiers and army apprentices up into the hills of Snowdonia, gave me a deep love and appreciation of their beauty. I explored the near pathless rocky and rugged Rhinogs, took them over Cader Idris in all its glory, and played follow my leader over boulder-filled streams on the Arans.

In the nineties I was President of the Council for National Parks and throughout the decade I held the post visited each on several occasions. I always got in a walk but it was also good to learn so much more about all the cultural and political issues, and the challenges of striking a balance between the needs of the local population and that of conservation. I was particular fond of my visits to Snowdonia.

More recently still I had the honour of carrying the Olympic torch to the top of Snowdon. Balancing on the top of the trig point amongst a crowd of cheering well-wishers was an emotional moment and I found myself crying at the realisation of the importance to me of this symbolic act that took me all the way back to my roots, when I first visited Snowdonia and discovered the passion of my life 60 years before.

Nick's book, his photography and words, are beautiful and the maps that accompany his descriptions are brilliant. I will be using his work on my own walks to help me find the best spots for photography in Snowdonia, and I'm sure that it will help you to have great adventures in these hills that have brought me so much joy.

Sir Chris Bonington
The Lake District, October 2018

Introduction

When I was asked to write the book you are now holding I was filled with excitement at the prospect of bringing together three of my biggest passions: hill walking, writing about hill walking and mountain photography; a dream come true. That excitement was soon tempered by a realisation of the enormity of the task I had taken on. A quick look at the stats reveals that to complete all of the 15 main routes in this book – forgetting the other ten roadside locations for a moment – you would walk 104 miles and ascend 12,680 metres (or 41,604ft), which equates to one Everest with three-and-a-half Snowdons on top.

In order to obtain the several hundred photographs needed to illustrate the book I would have to walk all the routes many times in all four seasons. It has been a labour of love and has given me enormous pleasure although there were numerous occasions when I thought I would never get it finished. Daily enquiries of "When's the book coming out?" became a major source of annoyance, but two and a half years later, I am very relieved to be able to say "Here's my book, I hope you enjoy it!"

With the steady rise in the popularity of both hill walking and landscape photography *Photographing the Snowdonia Mountains* aims to inspire seasoned hill walkers to develop their own photographic potential and encourage accomplished and enthusiastic practitioners of the art to take their photography, quite literally, to a higher level.

In selecting the routes and locations for this book I have tried to spread them across the length and breadth of the national park. The classic mountains of the north are not to be missed but the inclusion of a few lesser known but equally satisfying expeditions should whet your appetite for photographic investigations away from the *honeypots*. Each walk has its own peculiar character and atmosphere but all will reward you with superlative mountain scenery.

During the course of this project I have come to realise – with more than a little sadness – that one lifetime alone is not nearly enough to get to know every corner of this beautiful area, and as such, a book like this can only scratch the surface. It does, however, serve as a solid foundation from which to begin your own journey of discovery, camera in hand, as you explore the many and varied delights that Snowdonia has in abundance.

With my work here nearly done, all that remains is for me to wish each and every one of you many happy days in the mountains of Snowdonia. If, on your travels, you happen to see a short bald fella standing behind a tripod on a ridge or summit during the golden hour, go and say hello, it might be me!

Nick Livesey
Capel Curig, October 2018

The Afon Dudodyn and a cloud capped Snowdon.
Canon 6D, 24-70mm at 24mm, ISO 100, 1/50 sec at f/8, 0.9 graduated filter.

Using the guide

Photographing the Snowdonia Mountains has been written and designed primarily as a planning tool and a source of inspiration rather than a pocket-sized field guide. Before I was fortunate enough to live in Snowdonia my mountain photography trips were planned using guidebooks for ideas on where to go, maps for charting routes and larger format 'coffee table' volumes to whet my appetite and get psyched photographically. Back then I would have welcomed a guide which brought all these elements together but it didn't exist so I had to write it myself!

This book has all the information you'll need to plan a walk to suit your mood, experience and energy levels. Described are: **The Walks** – fifteen mountain walks that are usually circular. **Roadside Locations and Shorter Walks** – ten shorter outings and locations, often by the road, some requiring a short walk.

Route descriptions

Each chapter starts with an introduction, a general overview of the route and some text to set the scene. Then follows a detailed route description to keep you on track with numbered and named viewpoint suggestions on what to photograph. It's a good idea to read the description and follow it on the accompanying map to familiarise yourself with the 'shape' of the day. It should be noted that many individual viewpoints can (with a little planning and study of the map) be visited without the need to complete an entire route.

Maps and Elevation Profiles

The mapping in this book has been painstakingly put together to provide an accurate two dimensional representation of the routes you will be following with extra symbols denoting parking areas, pubs, campsites and youth hostels etc. They are, however, no substitute for the appropriate Ordnance Survey maps which are essential whilst out on the hill. OL 17, OL 18 and OL 23 are required to complete all the routes in this book. Elevation profiles provide an 'at a glance' reference for the ups and downs that will be encountered along the way as well as total ascent and distance covered.

The Ordnance Survey Explorer series, 1:25 000 scale

OS Explorer OL17 Snowdon / Yr Wyddfa
OS Explorer OL18 Harlech, Porthmadog & Bala / Y Bala
OS Explorer OL23 Cadair Idris & Llyn Tegid

Map Key

Start / Finish — **Start** and **finish** of the walk with its
106m — **elevation** in metres

Route – where the described walk goes

Walkers – recommended direction of the walk

2 **Viewpoint** – corresponds to viewpoint in route descriptions

P **Parking**

Campsite

yha **Youth Hostel**

Pub

Cafe

Restaurant

Hotel

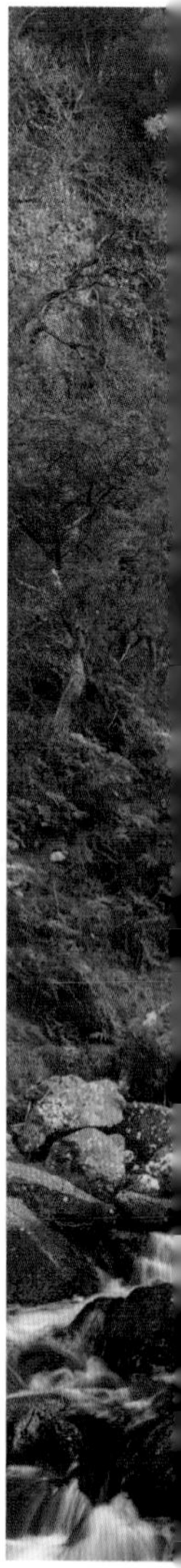

Hints of Autumnal colours at Aber Falls on an October afternoon. Canon 6D, 24-70mm at 37mm, ISO 100, 0.4 sec at f/13, polarising filter, tripod.

How to get here

Gwern Gof Isaf campsite lies on the main A5 trunk road and be easily accessed from the east – 7.5 miles from Betws y Coed – or the north, 7 miles from Bethesda.

Parking postcode: LL24 0EU
Parking grid ref: OS SH 66834 60518
Parking lat/long: 53.122225, -3.966162
Map: OS Explorer Map OL17 (1:25 000) Snowdon / Conwy Valley

Accessibility

This is a moderately strenuous high mountain walk of just under 11km with 800 metres of ascent. The paths are generally good but the area around Llyn y Caseg Fraith can be very boggy in all but prolonged periods of dry weather so gaiters are a useful addition to your kit. The ascent of Tryfan's South Ridge involves sections of very easy scrambling.

Best time of year/day

Braich y Ddeugwm, Llyn y Caseg Fraith and Y Foel Goch are wonderful year-round sunrise locations and usually very quiet while Tryfan and Cwm Bochlwyd are great for late light in the summer months. Under winter conditions Tryfan becomes a potentially serious climb that should not be attempted without an ice axe, crampons and experience in their use.

Grey Box Information

In the grey box of each chapter are the following:

How to get here

This paragraph includes directions and co-ordinates to the nearest parking place for each walk, and the required map needed for the walk.

Accessibility

This is a brief description of the terrain encountered on route often with snippets of advice.

Best time of year/day

Is sunset in autumn the best time for this walk?
Or is this walk good all-year round?
This paragraph will tell you.

Putting it all together

- Decide on your walk or location and read the relevant chapter in this book.
- Plan your route with this book, a paper map, and mapping apps or websites.
- Take a phone image of the relevant map in this book.
- Use Photographer's Ephemeris (**www.photoephemeris.com**) to find sunrise, sunset and golden hour times, and how the light will fall on the land.
- Make a sketch of your route and annotate with walk times (4km per hour plus one minute per 10 metres of ascent is a reasonable guestimate) and potential photography spots.
- Bring all of the above with you to North Wales. This book can stay in your car.

Camera, lenses and captions

Equipment

I have always viewed cameras and lenses as tools of the trade and have never lusted after the latest bit of kit or developed a gear fetish. With that in mind I keep my set up very simple and unless I have a specific shot in mind which requires extra equipment I take one lens (usually the 24-70mm) and one camera body with me when I'm out on the hill. Climbing mountains is hard enough as it is without carrying several kilograms worth of lenses on my back.

Since I started my photographic journey I have used graduated neutral density filters. Sensor technology may be improving all the time but I enjoy the craft element of using filters in the field and seeing an approximation of the final image on the back of my camera. There are still, of course, some effects which can't be replicated in post processing necessitating the use of filters such as a polariser and solid NDs. A tripod goes everywhere with me and over the years I have swung from using hulking great behemoths to the flimsiest examples which would struggle to hold an iphone. A compromise between these two extremes works best for me in terms of the performance to weight ratio.

Processing

My love for the landscapes of Snowdonia influences my style of processing which I aim to keep as natural looking as possible. From time to time an image may call for a more artistic treatment and in scenes of extreme contrast I may bracket 3 exposures and blend them together in Adobe Lightroom. Lightroom is the mainstay in my processing workflow but occasionally I move over to Photoshop for more detailed and precise editing. I like to preserve the integrity of a scene and use cloning/spot healing minimally and only to remove transient objects such as sheep droppings, stray vehicles or stubborn interlopers.

Equipment List

Camera Bodies
Canon 6D
Canon 7D
Canon G12 compact

Lenses
Canon EF 17-40mm f/4L USM
Canon EF 24-70mm f/4L IS USM
Canon EF 70-300mm f/4-5.6L IS USM

Filters
LEE soft graduated filters 0.3, 0.6 and 0.9
Kase K100-X filter holder
Kase slim circular polarising filter
Kase Wolverine 1.5 graduated filter
Kase Wolverine 6 stop neutral density filter

Tripod
Sirui ET-2004

Nick on Clip high above Cwm Bychan in the Rhinogydd.

Nick on Snowdon's Bwlch Main on a September evening.

Captions

It can be useful to know what camera and lenses photographers use, whether they used a tripod, what month they took the photograph in and what settings they used for exposure. By studying this information it can help our own photography. This comes with some caveats, the main one being that it is possible to take great photographs with the most basic of cameras and that there are always several choices of exposure variables.

There are two parts to the photographic captions in fotoVUE guidebooks.

VP 3. Foel Ddu rising out of the cloud from Moel yr Hydd – February afternoon.
Canon 6D, 24-70mm at 57mm, ISO 100, 1/200 sec at f/7.1, 0.6 graduated filter.

The Descriptive Caption

VP 3. Foel Ddu rising out of the cloud from Moel yr Hydd – February afternoon.

First is a descriptive caption that describes where the photograph was taken, mentions any references to viewpoints in the accompanying text, when the photograph was taken, and any other useful descriptive text.

Photographic Equipment and exposure settings

Canon 6D, 24-70mm at 57mm, ISO 100, 1/200 sec at f/7.1, 0.6 graduated filter.

The second part of the caption lists information describing the Camera, Lens, Exposure, Filter, Tripod or Handheld. Part of this information is the Exchangeable image file format (Exif data) that is recorded on the image file when you take a photograph.

Make and model of camera

Light–Exposure information
The ISO setting, shutter speed and aperture that the photograph was taken at.

Tripod or Handheld
If a tripod is used, it will say tripod. If not the photograph was taken by handholding the camera.

Canon 6D, 24-70mm at 24mm, ISO 100, 1/15 sec at f/11, 0.6 graduated filter, tripod.

Lens used and at what focal length

Filter used, if any

Snowdonia's mountain weather, climate and seasons

North Wales has a maritime climate being close to the sea, with weather that is often cloudy, wet and windy, and mild. The North Wales coast enjoys favourable conditions and experiences some of the highest temperatures in the UK year round. This contrasts with the nearby mountainous regions of Snowdonia, with several peaks over 1000m, which are often cloudy, cold and receive over 4000mm of rain a year – wetter than the Lake District or the Highlands of Scotland. Crib Goch received 6185 mm of rain (nearly 6.2 m) during 2015. My home village, Capel Curig, more often than not enjoys the accolade of wettest place in Britain.

In winter, snow, strong winds and freezing temperatures are frequent in the hills. Snowdon's summit (at 1085 metres) has an annual mean temperature of about 5 °C, with a mean daily minimum just above 0 °C in January. However, on some days in summer, shorts and a t-shirt are appropriate mountain wear, just make sure you have spare clothes and rain gear with you. The weather can change quickly in the mountains, one moment you can be clagged in by thick fog, the next, the fog will clear, the sun will burst through and you will be able to see right down to the coast.

Whilst in the valley it can be comfortable, as you ascend the temperature will decrease (known as the lapse rate), by as much as 1 °C per 100m, meaning if it is 10 °C in the valley it could be freezing on the tops. Be prepared for this.

Similarly with the wind, it will increase in strength as you ascend, with exposed ridges and 'bwlchs' or cols, frequently experiencing strong gusts that can knock you over. Combine strong wind, low temperatures with rain and conditions can be severe, even in summer.

Mountain valley weather averages

Met Office weather station at Capel Curig, Snowdonia
Location: 53.093, -3.941
Altitude: 216.0 m above mean sea level

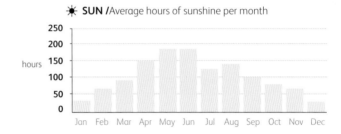

☀ **SUN /** Average hours of sunshine per month

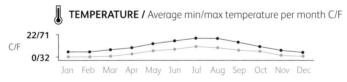

🌡 **TEMPERATURE /** Average min/max temperature per month C/F

❄ **FROST /** Average days of frost per month

	Jan	Feb	Mar	Apr	May	Jun	Jul	Aug	Sep	Oct	Nov	Dec
days	10	10	7	5	2	0	0	0	0	2	4	10

☁ **RAIN /** Average days rain/month and precipitation in mm

	Jan	Feb	Mar	Apr	May	Jun	Jul	Aug	Sep	Oct	Nov	Dec
mm	290	224	243	152	132	133	143	181	209	298	293	308

Local weather forecasts and conditions

Met Office – Snowdonia – Mountain weather forecast
www.metoffice.gov.uk/public/weather/mountain-forecasts/snowdonia

Mountain Weather Information Service
www.mwis.org.uk

Norwegian Weather Service: Yr and NRK
www.yr.no

BBC Weather Service
www.bbc.com/weather

Snowdonia weather cams

Snowdonia Weather and Webcam –
Live Webcam from Plas y Brenin
www.pyb.co.uk/weather/web-cam

Ogwen Valley Mountain Rescue
www.ogwen-rescue.org.uk

The White Spider
www.thewhitespider.com

Idwal Stream on a cold November morning. Canon 6D, 24-70mm at 70mm, ISO 100, 0.4 sec at f/11, tripod, polarising filter, 0.9 graduated filter.

Cat Evans enjoying a spring evening scramble on Y Gribin. Canon 6D, 24-70mm at 24mm, ISO 100, 1/60 sec at f/8, 0.6 graduated filter.

Moel Siabod and the Snowdon Range from Pen y Geuallt on an August evening. Six shot stitched panorama. Canon 7D, 17-40mm at 17mm, ISO 100, 1/5 sec at f/11, 0.9 graduated filter, tripod.

The Snowdonia mountains through the seasons

Spring – March, April, May

Like most areas in the UK spring can be a most productive time for landscape photography. On the mountain slopes, heather, bracken, sedges and grasses are still asleep in their brown, yellow and russet coats which contrast with a variety of shades of green as different species of trees and shrubs burst into leaf. On the higher peaks there may still be snow which adds even more contrast to mountain landscape photographs.

April showers and a higher sun bring changing light. Often there are settled spells of good weather with little moisture in the air. Storms come in quickly bringing in big white fluffy clouds. This is a good time for valley mists and temperature inversions with mountain peaks rising above a sea of cotton wool as far as the eye can see.

Summer – June, July, August

Summer is the driest period in North Wales accompanied by the highest number of hours sunshine. It will still rain, but during the day there are often clouds in the blue sky.

It is often hazy during the day in the peak summer months with air clarity at its lowest. Wild camping is recommended at this time of year – perhaps more so than any other.

It's common to see distinct cloud formations lining up above the Snowdonia mountains which appear to almost mirror the peaks; they look at their most photogenic during late evening when the clouds deflect the rays of the low evening sun onto the landscape below. When a mountain in Wales has cloud covering its summit it is said to be *gwisgo'i gap* or wearing it's cap.

Looking down the Llugwy Valley from Mynydd Garthmyn on a November morning. Canon 6D, 24-70mm at 35mm, ISO 100, 1/25 sec at f/8, 0.6 graduated filter, tripod.

Snowdon from Yr Aran on an evening in March. Canon 6D, 24-70mm at 24mm, ISO 100, 1/10 sec at f/11, 0.9 graduated filter, tripod.

Autumn – September, October, November

In October the bracken is well on its way to turning from green to brown to gold and the mountains and hills start to get more contrast which often coincides with the first snows.

The weather. Expect more rain and the first early morning frosts in October. Temperature inversions form mist in the valleys, during the day their may be periods of high pressure and clear sunny conditions. The days are getting shorter, the sun is low in the sky for most of the day and for many this is the best season for mountain photography before winter sets in properly.

Winter – December, January, February

In the midst of winter North Wales can be a grim place with high rainfall and grey cloud for days on end from the mountain tops to the sea. Unless you live locally or close-by December to February can be unproductive for landscape photography unless it snows. However this time of year, if you are lucky, can provide some of the best conditions for landscape photography, and sunrise is at a reasonable hour.

On average the mountains of Snowdonia get 30 days of snow a year. Typically the first snows are in early November but it can lie on the mountains any time between October and early May. The warmer coastal regions rarely get snow and if it does you'll get some unique photographs but it won't hang around too long at lower elevations. The mountains though can be draped in snow above 700m for long periods of time providing the perfect backdrop for landscape photography. Look out for a forecast of high pressure after it has snowed which should produce clear skies and good views of snowy peaks. Be prepared for snow to come and go though.

The sun and light

If you were standing on the summit of Snowdon on the 21st December, the shortest day and winter solstice, the sun would rise at 8.28am in the south east looking toward Capel Curig, then slowly travel across the southern horizon hardly reaching above 15 degrees above the horizon, and 7.5 hours later at 4pm the sun would set in the south west over the Llŷn Peninsula. In the winter, the north facing slopes barely get any sun, and narrow deep valleys are always in the shade. This is the time of year when the sun rises above Pen y Pass at the top of the Llanberis Pass, if you are standing in Llanberis.

Fast forward to the summer solstice, 21st June, the longest day and the sun rises at 4.50am in the north east, in the direction of Colwyn bay if you are on Snowdon's summit, then the sun arcs almost overhead and 16 hours later at 9.46pm it sets in the north east in the direction of Anglesey. This is the time of year when sunset aligns with looking down the Llanberis Pass, from Pen y Pass and similar if high on Tryfan or the Gyders looking down the Nant Ffrancon toward Bangor.

It's worth paying attention to where and when the sun is for all types of outdoor photography as it determines the quality of light, what is illuminated and hence the mood of your photographs.

When the sun is lower in the sky near sunrise and sunset, known as the golden hour, the light is soft and diffused, there is more contrast, the shadows are softer, the light warm and there is less chance of blown out highlights. Many prefer sunrise to sunset, despite the unearthly time of sunrise in the summer, as usually there is less haze and there is more chance of low lying mist and fog which adds atmosphere. Good photographic conditions can also last longer first thing. Both ends of the day benefit from having a little cloud above the horizon which can become colourfully illuminated.

As well as either end of the day, in late autumn into winter through to early spring, the sun is low in the sky for most of the day and the light a better quality than midday in summer. It can be worth staying out all day if conditions are good.

Another consideration is what the light falls upon, and studying a map, using the The Photographer's Ephemeris (**app.photoephemeris.com**) and experience in the field will be your best guide.

The sun position compass, sun elevation through the year graphic and the Sunrise/Sunset table shown opposite are a good starting if you need to learn more.

SUN POSITION COMPASS FOR SNOWDONIA

SUNRISE AND SUNSET POSITION THROUGH THE YEAR
on the 15th of each month

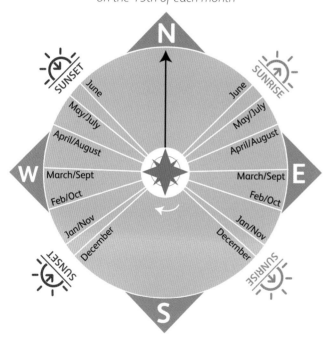

Either whilst in the field or planning with a map, orientate this book north/south and using the Sun Position Compass – you will get an approximate direction of where the sun will rise and set each month.
Data from The Llanberis Pass (53.08043°N 4.02135°W)

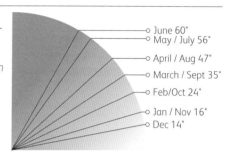

SUN ELEVATION THROUGH THE YEAR
The approximate elevation of the sun above the horizon (in degrees) at midday on the 15th of each month.

- June 60°
- May / July 56°
- April / Aug 47°
- March / Sept 35°
- Feb/Oct 24°
- Jan / Nov 16°
- Dec 14°

AVERAGE SUNRISE/SUNSET TIMES AND LENGTH OF DAYLIGHT HOURS

Month	Sunrise	Sunset	Daylight
January	8:22am	4:39pm	8:07hrs
February	7:33am	5:27pm	9:53hrs
March	6:31am	6:20pm	11:49hrs
April	6:17am	8:15pm	13:58hrs
May	5:17am	9:08pm	15:50hrs
June	4:49am	9:44pm	16:54hrs
July	5:08am	9:35pm	16:26hrs
August	5:56am	8:43pm	14:46hrs
September	6:49am	7:31pm	12:42hrs
October	7:42am	6:20pm	10:38hrs
November	7:39am	4:20pm	8:40hrs
December	8:23am	3:58pm	7:35hrs

Where to stay, eat and drink

The following are the most convenient bases from which to tackle the photographic walks in this book with a recommended selection of places to stay, eat, drink and be merry.

Regarding accommodation, I have listed hostels and campsites; for hotels, and bed & breakfast, check **www.airbnb.com** and **www.tripadvisor.com**

Capel Curig and Betws y Coed

Best bases for Moel Siabod, Crimpiau, The Carneddau, The Glyderau, the Tour of Tryfan, Cwm Idwal (roadside), Pen yr Ole Wen (roadside), Llynnau Mymbyr (roadside) and Foel Berfedd (roadside).

Cafes and Chippies

Moel Siabod Café	LL24 0EL
Nemo Chippy	LL24 0AE
Alpine Café	LL24 0AE
Pont y Pair Chippy	LL24 0BN

Pubs

Tyn y Coed Hotel	LL24 0EE
Bryn Tyrch Inn	LL24 0EL

The Stables	LL24 0AY
Pen y Gwryd Hotel	LL55 4NT

Accommodation

Swallow Falls YHA	LL24 0EW
Pen y Pass YHA	LL55 4NY
The Rocks at Plas Curig independent hostel	LL24 0EL
Dolgam Campsite	LL24 0DS
Garth Farm Campsite	LL24 0ES
Gwern Gof Isaf Campsite	LL24 0EU

Llanberis

Best base for The Snowdon Horseshoe, The Round of Marchlyn Mawr, Moel Eilio, Moel y Ci (roadside) and the Llanberis Pass (roadside).

Cafes and Chipies

Pete's Eats	LL55 4EU
Alports Chippy (closes 9pm)	LL55 4EU
Pen Ceunant Isaf Tea House	LL55 4UW
Llygad y Haul Cafe	LL55 4SU

Pubs

The Heights (closes 10.30pm)	LL55 4HB
The Vaynol Arms	LL55 4UF
Padarn Hotel	LL55 4SU
Gallt y Glyn Pizza and a Pint	LL55 4EL

Accommodation

Llanberis YHA	LL55 4SR

Ben's Bunkhouse	LL55 4UD
Ty Isaf Campsite	LL55 4UN
Llanberis Campsite & Glamping Yurts	LL55 4SR

Dolgellau and Barmouth

Best bases for Cadair Idris and Llynnau Cregennan.

Cafes and Chippies

The Dolphin Fish Bar (closes 8.30pm)	LL42 1AD
The Cosy Take Away	LL40 1LN
Y Sospan	LL40 1AW
Murray's Cafe Bar	LL42 1AN

Pubs

The Last Inn	LL42 1EL
The Royal Ship Hotel	LL40 1AR
Yr Unicorn	LL40 1ES
The Stag Inn	LL40 1AU

Accommodation

Kings YHA	LL40 1TB
Bunkorama	LL42 1DX
Byncws HYB Bunkhouse	LL40 1AU
Torrent Walk Campsite	LL40 2AB
Hafod Dywyll Campsite	LL40 1TR

Beddgelert and Rhyd Ddu

Best bases for The Nantlle Ridge, Moel y Dyniewyd, The Nantmor Skyline, Nant Gwynant (roadside), Carreg Hylldrem (roadside) and Llyn y Dywarchen (roadside).

Cafes and Chippies

Hebog Eat	LL55 2UY
Glaslyn Ices	LL55 4YB
Ty Mawr Tea Room	LL55 6TL
Caffi Colwyn	LL55 4YA

Pubs

Tanronnen Inn	LL55 4YB
Prince Llewelyn Hotel	LL55 4LT
The Saracen's Head Hotel	LL55 4UY
The Cwellyn Arms	LL55 6TL

Accommodation

Bryn Gwynant YHA	LL55 4NP
Snowdon Ranger YHA	LL55 7YS
Beddgelert Campsite	LL55 4UU
Cae Du Campsite	LL55 4NE
Llyn Gwynant Campsite	LL55 4NW

Llanbedr and Harlech

Best bases for Rhinog Fawr.

Cafes and Chippies

Harlech Fish and Chips Shop	LL46 2YB
Castle Pizza and Kebab House	LL46 2YB
Caffi Castell (closes 5pm)	LL46 2YH
The Old Bakery (closes 8pm)	LL45 2LD

Pubs

Y Branwen LL46 2PU

The Victoria Inn LL45 2LD

Accommodation

Dinas Caravan and Camping Park LL45 2PH

Nantcol Waterfalls Campsite LL45 2PL

Bunkorama LL42 1DX

Byncws HYB Bunkhouse LL40 1AU

Bala

Best base for Arenig Fawr.

Cafes and Chippies

Tegid Cafe LL23 7LG

Y Badell Aur LL23 7AF

Plas yn Dre Ty Coffi LL23 7AG

The Loch Cafe LL23 7SR

Pubs

The Bull's Head LL23 7AD

The Ship LL23 7AD

The Eagles Inn LL23 7UB

The Bryntirion Inn LL23 7RA

Accommodation

Bala Backpackers Hostel LL23 7EL

Bala Bunkhouse LL23 7HD

Ty Isaf Campsite LL23 7PP

Ty Cornel Campsite LL23 7NU

Blaenau Ffestiniog, Tanygrisiau and Maentwrog

Best base for the Moelwynion.

Cafes and Chippies

Lakeside Cafe LL41 3TP

The Bridge Cafe LL41 3HD

Ian's Fish restaurant LL41 3ES

Blaenau Take Away LL41 3DB

Pubs

Meirion Vaults LL41 3AE

Manod Hotel LL41 3LJ

The Oakeley Arms Hotel LL41 3YU

The Grapes Hotel LL41 4HN

Accommodation

Hostel Cellb LL41 3AD

Treks Bunkhouse LL41 4PS

Llechrwd Campsites LL41 4HF

Middle left: The Moel Siabod Cafe, Capel Curig.

Bottom: The historic Pen y Gwryd Hotel backed by Glyder Fach

Mountain gear

Being kitted out with a functional clothing system should be a priority when heading into the hills. If the weather turns nasty your comfort and more importantly your safety will depend on it. Outdoor kit has come a long way since the Victorian pioneers set about exploring the mountains in tweeds and nailed boots and although there is a vast range of makes, models and price points available most gear on sale today will do the job to a larger or lesser degree.

That said, I have yet to find anything that would keep me dry for long in horizontal rain in the Carneddau but sometimes a little discomfort is a price I pay during adventurous photographic outings. Britain's maritime climate dictates that sometimes we may get a little clammy or even very wet but the main function of modern gear is regulating temperature using the layering system.

The Layering System

- Base layers are the foundation on which the system is based. T shirts and underwear made from polypropylene or merino wool dry quickly and have a wicking action which transports sweat away from the body. Garments made from cotton should not be worn as when they become wet they stay wet which leads to rapid cooling.

- Mid layers come in several forms. A traditional fleece jacket provides warmth and retains heat when wet but offers little protection from the wind. Trousers and jackets made from soft-shell are a good choice and provide much better wind resistance than fleece but can hold on to moisture when wet despite claims of being shower proof.

- Down or synthetic fill jackets are far to warm to be used when active but come into their own during periods of rest or immobility and should be considered essential for those long vigils which occur when waiting for the light.

- Hard shell clothing for top and bottom is designed to keep out the weather with modern fabrics such as Gore-Tex and eVent offering varying degrees of breathability. Should a hard shell 'wet out' it will lose its ability to breath and you will become damp from condensation but they are extremely wind resistant which helps to keep you warm when on the move.

Footwear

There are those who love to travel light favouring trail/ approach shoes when in the hills and they are growing in number although the vast majority of hill goers still opt for boots which are rated from B0 (flexible) to B3 (fully rigid for technical ice climbing). My preference has long been to wear B1 boots in summer and B2 in winter which allow all day crampon use. The boots you choose will depend on your own preferences and what you plan to do in them but the crucial thing is that they fit correctly. Before deciding on a purchase it is very wise to visit a reputable outdoor shop for boot fitting and expert advice.

Mountain gear

Extremities

When it gets cold the body moves heat away from the extremities to protect the core which results in cold fingers, toes, ears and nose. This can be very uncomfortable and even dangerous in winter conditions. If you have ever lost the feeling in your fingers then it is a small leap to imagine how difficult it will be to control your camera and attach filters during a cold shoot. Make sure you take the following with you and carry spares ...

- Beanie hat
- Gloves (two pairs)
- Buff
- Good quality socks such as those made by Bridgedale

Rucksack

You can purchase specially designed hill walking camera backpacks from Lowe Pro or F-Stop. They have a camera carrying system internally and plenty of non-camera storage for your spare clothes and food/drink, as well as internal frame and comfortable carrying straps. They are expensive however and most people do adequately well with a standard mountain day sack of around 40L in capacity. Inserting foam padding internally to protect you camera and lenses is advised rather than having them floating free amongst your rain jacket, sandwiches and flask. Waterproof drysacks are a good idea to protect and organise the gear in your rucksack. Using a hip holster to carry your camera is also useful.

Winter Essentials

In winter the mountains become a much more serious proposition and including some specialist kit in your armoury is non negotiable.

An ice axe must be carried if there is any suggestion of snow or ice on the tops accompanied by crampons (C1–C2 or C3 rated) which are matched to the boots you will be using. It's worth pointing out that 'bendy' (B0) boots are entirely unsuitable for winter mountains with B1 rated boots considered an absolute minimum. In the wrong hands axe and crampons can be extremely dangerous so it is recommended that their use is coupled with the requisite experience which can be gained by hiring a guide or going on a winter skills course.

Micro-spikes are recommended if there is any chance of sub-zero conditions and on level or moderately inclined iced-up slopes they are superior to crampons for walking in. Micro-spikes fit on any type of footwear.

Eye protection is an important consideration especially on bright days when reflected light can damage your eyesight. It's also worth packing ski goggles to preserve vision in the event of a blizzard.

Gaiters are very useful in winter as they will prevent snow entering your boots.

Take inner and outer gloves with you, and a spare pair. Hand Warmers sachets are very useful, providing up to 7 hours of warmth; pop one in a pocket or glove with your spare battery to extend battery life.

Mountain safety

In lowland and easily accessible areas you may at times get wet, cold and miserable; you may experience a memory card failure or the pain of an early rise. These are usually the worst things you will have to contend with in your landscape photography. When out photographing in the mountains the stakes are much higher. Getting to and from your locations safely is something that should be given serious consideration before you head out into the hills.

The mountains of Snowdonia can be unforgiving places for those without the experience or equipment to cope with the rough terrain, changeable weather and poor visibility often met at higher elevations. Unlike roadside photography where, if things turn nasty you can bail out quickly, when high on a mountain you will be committed and possibly two or three hours away from the safety of your car and a nice warm pub. Although an extensive guide to mountain safety is beyond the remit of this book the following chapter will give you an idea of some of the potential hazards you may come across in the course of your photographic journeys in Snowdonia along with suggestions on how best to approach them.

Mountain Weather
"Even in the summer months it is not unusual to experience four seasons in one day."

The biggest factor influencing both the ground conditions and your wellbeing on the hill is the weather, which can range from a scorching day of clear blue skies in July to a full-blown whiteout in winter. Both scenarios can be debilitating and represent extremes which bookend every other combination of atmospheric phenomena possible in the mountain environment. Indeed, even in the summer months it is not unusual to experience four seasons in one day and it is important to have protective clothing to protect you from these extremes.

It is vitally important before embarking on an expedition to obtain a reliable forecast not just to assess the chance of suitable photographic conditions but more importantly to get a good idea of whether or not it is safe to head high for a day out with your camera.

There are a myriad of mobile phone apps available but a good place to start for detailed mountain weather forecasts are the **Met Office and MWIS (Mountain Weather Information Service)** websites which are updated 365 days a year and are relied upon by many thousands of hill walkers and climbers in the UK. Weather forecasting is by its very nature an inexact science but in this day and age there is no excuse for blundering blindly into the eye of a storm unless a potentially serious tussle with the elements is what you're after and that, of course, is usually incompatible with capturing great images.

Scrambling
Scrambling is the grey area between a simple walk at one end of the spectrum and easy rock climbing at the other although the word easy in this context is misleading in that for most it would involve specialist equipment and experience in its use. Within this book are a small number of routes which contain sections of Grade 1 scrambling where the use of hands as well as feet will be required to make progress but where a fall could result in serious injury or death.

On a day of light winds and dry rock these routes should be well within the capabilities of experienced and steady hill walkers possessing a good head for heights. In high winds, rain or a combination of both they should be treated with extreme caution and ideally avoided. This tactic of avoidance especially applies to periods when there is snow and ice on the hills. At these times the routes become graded winter climbs and are only suitable for experienced and well equipped mountaineers.

Keep in mind that mountains are in a perpetual state of decay and the quality of the rock shouldn't be taken for granted. Always test the integrity of hand and foot holds before committing your weight to them.

Crib Goch in winter, no place for the inexperienced. **Below:** *Scrambling on Snowdon's Gribin Ridge.*

For the purpose of this book, in good conditions *The tour of Tryfan* is an ideal introductory route on which to try your hand at scrambling while *The Snowdon Horseshoe* sits at the upper end of seriousness and technical difficulty to be found in these pages. It's worth bearing in mind that these scrambles won't disappear any time soon so if in any doubt you should work your way through the easier but photographically no less rewarding routes until your experience matches your ambition.

Going it Alone

Landscape photography can be a solitary pursuit and nowhere is that solitude more profoundly felt *and* enjoyed than in the mountain environment. There are those that enjoy company and the camaraderie of fellow photographers but for me and many others there is nothing better than being alone on a mountain summit, waiting for the break of day and the promise of wonderful light in which to record an unrepeatable and unique moment in time.

The received wisdom is that unless you are very experienced then it is a good idea to go with a friend or two in case of emergency. The obvious danger of going alone in the hills is that you may injure yourself and be unable to continue your journey back home without help, possibly succumbing to shock or/and hypothermia. Less immediately dramatic perhaps but still potentially serious is getting lost during periods of poor visibility which can occur rapidly and with little prior warning. To find yourself in this situation is a frightening experience and can lead to a night out on the hill or wandering onto dangerous terrain.

Digital mapping, GPS units and mobile phone apps are getting better all the time but can fail and shouldn't be relied upon to get you out of trouble. An Ordnance Survey or Harvey map for the area you are operating in and a good compass will not let you down. Navigation with map and compass is an essential skill for anyone walking in the mountains but takes time and practise to master. There are many good books available on the subject as well as navigation courses where you can learn all the relevant techniques to safely find your way through the hills whatever the weather.

Mountain safety

Route Planning

Planning a photography walk in the mountains will involve a combination of consulting weather forecasts, studying maps, considering the right time of day and year for the best light. The result should be an expedition suitable for your ability, fitness and photographic aspirations.

There is a lot to think about before donning your boots and strapping on your pack. I have walked and photographed all the routes and locations in this book many times. The descriptions have been checked for accuracy and will provide you with all the information you need regarding what you can expect to photograph, the terrain encountered along with time saving local knowledge such as where to park the car and how to get there. As far as is possible the hard work of route planning has been taken out of the equation.

However, planning your own days out is an extremely rewarding exercise and the following walks can be used as templates for further exploration and devising your own itineraries. Once you have settled on your route it is good practice to fill out a *route card* and leave it with a responsible person. For a downloadable route card and further detailed information **www.mountainsafety.co.uk** is a fantastic resource for anyone taking to the mountains.

If the Worst Happens

Should you get into difficulties it is important to know how to summon help. In the days before mobile phones hill goers finding themselves in trouble used the international distress signal of six blasts on a whistle repeated with an interval of one minute between each series of six blasts. The same technique can be used with flashes from a torch. As most now take a mobile phone onto the hill it is more usual to call for help from mountain rescue, a decision which should not be taken lightly.

To do this dial **999** or **112**, ask for police and then mountain rescue. Then be ready to give a **CHALET** report.

C **Casualties** – number, names (and, if possible, age); type of injuries, for example, lower leg, head injury, collapse, drowning etc.

H **Hazards** to the rescuers – for example, strong winds, avalanche, rock fall, dangerous animals.

A **Access** – the name of mountain area and description of the terrain. It may be appropriate to describe the approach and any distinguishing features such as an orange survival bag. Information on the weather conditions at the incident site is useful, particularly if you are in cloud or mist.

L **Location** of the incident – a grid reference and a description is ideal. Don't forget to give the map sheet number and please say if the grid reference is from a GPS device.

E **Equipment** at the scene – for example, torches, other mobile phones, group shelters, medical personnel.

T **Type** of incident – mountain, aircraft, train, etc. Be prepared to give a brief description of the time and apparent cause of the incident.

North Wales Mountain Rescue

There are eight search and rescue teams in North Wales. The Llanberis Mountain Rescue Team is the busiest in the UK with nearly 200 incidents a year, primarily on Snowdon. The neighbouring Ogwen Valley Mountain Rescue Organisation are focussed on the peaks lining the Ogwen Valley. The South Snowdonia Search and Rescue covers the Rhinogydd, Arenig and Moelwyn mountains, and Aberdyfi Search and Rescue Team cover Cader idris, Aran Fawddwy and Pumlumon.

Find out more about these teams and donate at the North Wales Mountain Rescue Association website **www.nwmra.org**

Courses

The National Mountain Sports Centre at Plas y Brenin in Capel Curig run a range of mountain courses including Hill Skills, Navigation and Scrambling. They are highly recommended. **www.pyb.co.uk**

Alternatively you can find a mountain instructor at **www.mountain-training.org** or a mountain guide at **www.bmg.org.uk**

Checking the map in deteriorating conditions.

Wild camping

For those seeking to make the very most of their trips to the mountains a wild camp high in the hills is a great way to maximise shooting opportunities when the light is likely to be at its best. By encouraging you to slow down your in the field workflow, camping wild affords a greater appreciation of your surroundings and allows you to really hone those all important compositions.

Your photography needn't be confined to the golden hours either with clear nights offering excellent scope for astro photography. The advantages of spending a night under the stars are, however, offset by the heavy burden on your back but two bites of the golden hour cherry is a powerful incentive for those willing to put in the extra effort. Wild camping also removes the need for walking during the hours of darkness which can be a source of anxiety for less experienced mountain photographers.

Legality

The legal position on wild camping in Snowdonia (and the rest of England and Wales) is clear cut in that it is forbidden unless permission is given by the landowner. The official stance, however, is not as hopeless as it may appear and there is a long tradition of tolerance towards discreet camping in the mountains. Problems occur when this tacit agreement is abused by irresponsible practices and inconsiderate behaviour. In the first instance permission should be sought and information on the relevant landowner for your camp can be obtained from the Snowdonia National Park authority. If for whatever reason this is not possible then common sense and due consideration should suffice 9 times out of 10.

Responsible Wild Camping

Wild camping may not be a legal right in England and Wales but a code of conduct/best practice has developed over time throughout the outdoor community. A 'leave not trace' ethic is paramount if you are to wild camp responsibly, "take nothing but photographs, leave nothing but footprints" is the perfect maxim to carry with you on your travels.

- Aim to site your camp above the intake wall of the mountain and out of sight of any roads.
- Keep group numbers small.
- Pitch your tent at dusk and break camp at dawn.
- Don't not camp in the same location for more than one night.
- Do not light fires.
- Do not go to the toilet within 40 metres of streams or lakes.
- Bury human waste in a hole at least 15cm deep or, ideally, carry it out with you.
- Leave the site exactly as you found it. Should you need to move rocks then return them to their original position after use.
- If you wash in streams or lakes then use the water alone. Any kind of soap is a pollutant that can alter the chemical composition of the local habitat.
- And finally, enjoy your wild camping.

Opposite top: A cold April camp on Glyder Fach. 8 shot stitched panorama. © Kris Williams. *Sony A7s, 16-35mm at 16mm, ISO 6400, 25 sec at f/2.8, tripod.*

Middle: An April dusk on Glyder Fach backed by the Snowdon range. © Helen Iles. *Nikon D750, 24-70mm at 24mm, ISO 640, 24mm at f/5.6, tripod.*

Bottom: Paul Hodges enjoying a warming brew in the shadow of Tryfan on a September wild camp beside Llyn y Caseg Fraith. *Canon 6D, 24-70 at 24mm, ISO 200, 1/40 sec at f/8, 0.6 graduated filter.*

Kit

Along with your usual hill walking gear and photography equipment you will need to take some extra kit with you and a rucksack big enough to carry it all in. An acceptable level of comfort varies from person to person with some willing to rough it in a bivi bag or under a tarp to keep their pack weight down. My personal preference is to be as comfortable as possible with a load not exceeding 15kg. It takes a bit of practise to settle on a system that works for you but below is a list of essential items I take with me on my wild camping trips.

- Osprey Aether 70ltr backpack
- Hilleberg AKTO four season mountain tent
- Therm-a-Rest NeoAir XLite sleeping mat
- A season appropriate sleeping bag packed into an exped dry bag
- MSR Pocket Rocket Stove
- Light weight cook set and two plastic sporks
- Food for an evening meal and light breakfast
- Ear plugs for camps in windy conditions
- Hand warmers for colder camps
- A good bottle of red wine decanted into a hydration bladder or hip flask of single malt whiskey
- Reading material for autumn and winter camps
- A head torch and plenty of spare batteries

Planning a photographic day on the hill

I've been photographing in the mountains for so long now that when I plan a shoot it is done with very little conscious thought. I have the routine dialled in so instinctively that I go through the various stages of preparation almost automatically from 'sofa to summit' and back again. For the benefit of those with less experience of mountain photography I'll take you through my approach and break it down into four steps.

Which location?

It might sound obvious but before I set out I need to decide where I'm going to go. Wandering around aimlessly is an exciting way to work if you're well practiced in being reactive when good light suddenly presents itself but a sound plan coupled with a bit of patience will stack the odds in your favour of coming away with a good image. My choice of location is always informed by how the light might fall upon it during my preferred time frame, be it sunrise, sunset or even in the middle of the day. More often than not I'll favour a scene which is side lit and with that in mind I'll consult the 'Photographer's Ephemeris' to ascertain whether or not the shots I have in mind have a chance of coming to fruition. It may be that my chosen location won't be ripe for a few weeks or even months and that being the case I'll find somewhere else to go. Having some idea of how long it will take to reach your location is essential if you are to arrive in time for that once in a lifetime lightshow. 4km per hour plus one minute per 10 metres of ascent is a reasonable guestimate. Walking a route you are unfamiliar with and/or in the dark will add time onto your approach so it's wise to factor in some leeway.

Weather

I've decided on my location and now it's time to take a look at what the weather might do. This would appear to be a no-brainer, is it a goer or is it not? If only it were that simple. There are times when various weather forecasts/apps disagree with each other and if you use multiple sources to gather weather information and a consensus isn't met then it's always going to be a leap of faith. Changeable weather can lead to dramatic images but when conditions look marginal I'm more likely to take a chance on sunset rather than sunrise for reasons which will become apparent if you've dragged yourself out of bed to climb a 3000ft mountain in the dark more than once only to be met with an opaque wall of clag.

Kit and day before

If it's looking good and I've decided where to go I'll then make sure my kit is ready for action. Faffing at the last minute introduces stress into your day and can result in forgetting essential items. The night before my shoot I'll charge my camera batteries and clean my lenses and filters as well as making sure my memory cards (always take a spare!) are formatted. I'll also check my tripod, tighten any loose screws and strap it to my pack.

My hill walking kit falls into three categories, clothing, smalls and sustenance. I like to lay my clothes out the night before and try to wear as little as possible at the start of my walk. With that in mind my insulted jacket and waterproofs are stashed away until they are needed. Once I get walking I quickly warm up and starting out chilly means I don't have to stop to remove layers. Smalls live in the lid of my rucksack and include a headtorch (fully charged/spare batteries), hat and gloves (I take several spares), compass, the correct map, a whistle and a small first aid kit. If using a small lunch box then food can be stored in any available cranny of your pack. Unprotected sandwiches, however, have a nasty habit of becoming hideously deformed if not stored sympathetically! When walking to or from a location, nibbles kept in your pocket help with moral and give an energy boost on the go if required.

I aim to have everything packed in my rucksack so it can be picked up and slung into the car at a moment's notice which is especially important if going for a sunrise. It's also a very good idea to leave your boots next to your rucksack. More than once I have had to turn back half way to my location because in a zombie-like pre-dawn state I have neglected to pick them up! How you pack your rucksack is down to personal preference but think about the order in which you will use your kit and pack accordingly.

Above: Nick photographing dawn on Crib Goch. © Dave Dear. *Below*: Dave's sandwich. © Dave Dear

Using drybags helps with organisation and also keeps out moisture if the weather turns foul. Managing your kit in an efficient and methodical way will save time and enable you to focus on your photography when conditions are giving it the big one, don't just throw it all in and hope for the best.

On location planning

So, I've arrived at my location safe and sound, allowing myself plenty of time to get sorted out before the show starts. If it's chilly then the first thing I'll do is put on extra layers, have a drink and something to eat while taking in the sights and sounds. Before I even think about getting my camera out I'll explore my immediate surroundings and look for compositions. When I find a promising spot I'll set my gear up and work the composition by incrementally moving my camera left and right, back and forth, up and down, until I have maximised the potential of the scene in front of me. At this point I'll ask myself a few questions; what filters (if any) should I use? Is the dynamic range of the scene such that I'll need to bracket? Is lens flare going to be an issue? Is the wind speed low enough to capture a sharp image without adjusting my ISO? Once I'm happy I'll take some test shots to make sure that everything is as it should be. It is then a case of waiting for the light but 'insurance shots' should be taken at intervals. It is not unusual for conditions to crap out at the last minute leaving you with nothing to show for all the effort you've put in. During outstanding light events try to resist the urge to capture as many different images as possible. Flapping is an approach that almost always leads to frustration when, back at home, you find that although the light was great your compositions are weak and ill thought out. Experience has taught me that coming away with one solid image is much better than dozens of near misses.

And finally …

If your shoot has been a success you will no doubt be very excited and eager to get back home to work on your images. Be mindful that you're only halfway through getting the job done. Many accidents in the mountains happen on the descent when people are tired and 'switch off'. Take it easy and make getting down safely your priority.

Planning a photographic day on the hill

Planning tick list

1 Which location?
- Decide on your walk.
- Plan your route with this book, a paper map, and mapping apps or websites.
- Take a phone image of the relevant map in this book.
- Use Photographer's Ephemeris (**www.photoephemeris.com**) to find sunrise, sunset and golden hour times, and how the light will fall on the land.
- Make a sketch of your route and annotate with walk times (4km per hour plus one minute per 10 metres of ascent is a reasonable guestimate) and potential photography spots.

2 Weather
- Check the forecast a few days before and the day before.
- Recommended weather apps include: **www.yr.no** – a weather app from the *Norwegian Meteorological Institute* and *NRK*. The met office website/app, **www.metoffice.gov.uk**
- Changeable weather often brings great light, check for that sun symbol appearing amongst dark cloud and rain symbols in the weather forecast.

3 Kit and day before
- Charge camera batteries, bring fully charged spares.
- Clean lenses and filters.
- Format memory cards, bring spares.
- Pack rucksack or camera bag with camera gear and spare, warm, clothing – smalls hats and gloves.
- Pack a headtorch with spare batteries.
- Pack compass, the correct map, your notes, a whistle and a small first aid kit.
- Lay out clothing.
- Pack.
- Have change for any parking fees.

4 On location planning
- Keep warm and fed, it will improve your photography.
- Scan the location with your eyes and by looking through the viewfinder for compositions: amongst other compositional elements look for foreground, mid-ground and background, foreground anchor points (boulders, slabs, rocks, foliage), receding layers of hills, balance, symmetry, asymmetry, lines of hills that lead to a focal point.
- Consider dynamic range – do you need a ND grad or will you exposure blend? Either can work.
- Handheld or tripod? What are the light levels like? Is there a string wind?
- Take some test and insurance shots.
- Is the light good, will it change?
- Don't flap. If the light is great and conditions appear to be fleeting make sure you compose well. The rushed and scatter gun approach may work, but one well composed shot is worth a hundred 'not quite there' images.
- Stay safe and keep warm. Don't rush the walk back to the road when you are tired. Accidents happen on rushed descents.

The Welsh language – Cymraeg

Cymraeg is a beautiful and ancient language. Most who visit Wales find the long words seemingly devoid of vowels adorning road signs, shops and houses, unintelligible. If the written word is hard enough to decipher then the alien sounds of spoken Welsh compound the issue and leave many visitors mangling place names left, right and centre.

As an English man living in Wales and a student of Cymraeg, my life in Snowdonia has been greatly enriched by learning something of the language and over time mastering the pronunciation of place names and the mountains I climb. When one realises that the Welsh alphabet is not quite the same as its English counterpart (Welsh has at least two more vowels than English) things become a little easier to deal with. In Snowdonia National Park, Cymraeg is the first language of the majority of its inhabitants with 59% identifying as Welsh speakers. An authoritative guide to Welsh is beyond the scope of this book but this short summary of pronunciation and a glossary of useful Welsh words should help you get your tongue around Moel Ysgyfarnogod and open up the lyrical nature of Welsh mountain names.

Vowel Sounds

Short

a	as in Cat
e	as in Pen
i	as in Sing
o	as in Pot
u	as in Bin
w	as in Sum
y	as in Win

Long

a	as in Car
e	as in Dare
i	as in Keen
o	as in Pour
u	as in Dream
w	as in Cool
y	as in Seen

Consonants

b	as in Bell
c	as in Comb
ch	as in Loch
d	d
dd	as in There
f	as in Of
ff	as in Off
g	g
ng	as in Ring
h	h
l	l
ll	formed by placing the tongue on the roof of the mouth and saying thl
m	m
n	n
p	p
ph	ph
r	a rolled r sound
rh	pronounce the h before a rolled r
s	as in Sign
si	as in Shape
t	t
th	as in think

Caernarfon Castle.

Glossary

aber	river mouth		**glas**	blue
aderyn	bird		**gwyn/gwen**	white
afon	river		**gwynt**	wind
aran	high place		**hafod**	summer dwelling place
bach/fach	small or little		**haul**	sun
bryn	hill		**hen**	old
bwlch	pass		**hendre**	winter dwelling place
cadair	chair		**isaf**	lower or lowest
cae	field		**llan**	church/parish
capel	chapel		**lloer**	moon
carnedd	cairn		**llwyd**	grey
castell	castle		**llyn**	lake
cefn	ridge		**maes**	field
clogwyn	cliff/crag		**main**	narrow
coch/goch	red		**mawr/fawr**	big
coed	wood		**moel/foel**	bare hill
craig	crag		**mynydd**	mountain
crib	ridge/arete		**nant**	stream/valley
cwm	hollow/valley		**perfedd**	middle
dinas	fortress		**pont/bont**	bridge
drws	door		**rhyd**	ford
du/ddu	black		**saethau**	arrows
dwr	water		**ty**	house
dyffryn	valley		**uchaf**	upper or highest
ffynnon	spring, well			
ffridd	grazing enclosure			

The Welsh language – Cymraeg

Mountain Translations

Welsh mountain names are almost as old as the hills themselves reflecting the history of Wales and the inextricable link between the landscape and folklore of a nation steeped in myth and legend. While some are merely descriptive of the topography, many are touched with magic and evoke a time when stories were passed on in an oral tradition which survives to this day. It is not possible to accurately translate every name you will find in these pages as some are very old indeed and use words which have fallen out of usage or have mutated beyond recognition but here are some to get you started as you immerse yourself in mynyddoedd Eryri, the Snowdonia mountains.

Mountains/mynyddoedd

Pen yr Ole Wen	Head of the white light
Carnedd Dafydd	Dafydd's Cairn
Carnedd Llewelyn	Llewelyn's Cairn
Pen yr Helgi Du	Head of the black hound
Carnedd y Filiast	Cairn of the greyhound bitch
Mynydd Perfedd	Mountain of the intestines
Elidir Fawr (Carnedd Elidir)	Elidir's Cairn
Glyder Fach	The little pile
Glyder Fawr	The big plle
Y Garn	The Tumulus
Y Foel Goch	The bare red hill
Tryfan	Three rocks
Crib Goch	Red Ridge
Garnedd Ugain	Cairn of the twenty
Yr Wyddfa (Snowdon)	The Grave
Moelwyn Mawr	Big bare white hill

Mynydd Dwrs y Coed	Mountain at the door of the wood
Trum y Ddysgl	Ridge of the dish
Cnicht	Knight
Rhinog Fawr	The big threshold
Cadair Idris	Idris' chair
Pan y Gadair	The head of the chair
Moel y Ci	Bare hill of the dog
Pared y Cefn Hir	The long back wall

Lakes/llynnoedd

Ffynnon Lloer	Spring of the moon
Llyn y Cwn	The dog lake
Llyn y Caseg Fraith	Lake of the piebald mare
Llyn Coryn	Crown Lake
Llyn Llydaw	Lake Brittany
Llyn Du'r Arddu	Lake of the black height
Llyn Dinas	Lake of the fortress
Llyn yr Adar	The bird lake
Llynnau Cerrig y Myllt	Lakes of the sultry stone
Llyn Morwynion	Lake of the maiden
Gloyw lyn	The Gleaming lake
Llyn Du	The black lake
Llyn y Gadair	Lake of the chair
Llyn y Dywarchen	Lake of the floating sod

Moel Siabo

— MOELWYNION —

Northern Snowdonia from Nebo on a February evening.

— SNOWDON MASSIF — — GLYDERAU — — CARNEDDAU —

Garnedd Ugain

Snowdon

Glyder Fach Tryfan Elidir Fawr Pen yr Ole Wen

Carnedd Dafydd

Carnedd Llewelyn

Pen Llithrig yr Wrach

Foel Grach

Foel Fras

Llanberis Pass

Ogwen Valley

Glyder Fawr

Crimpiau Craig Wen

Creigiau Gleision

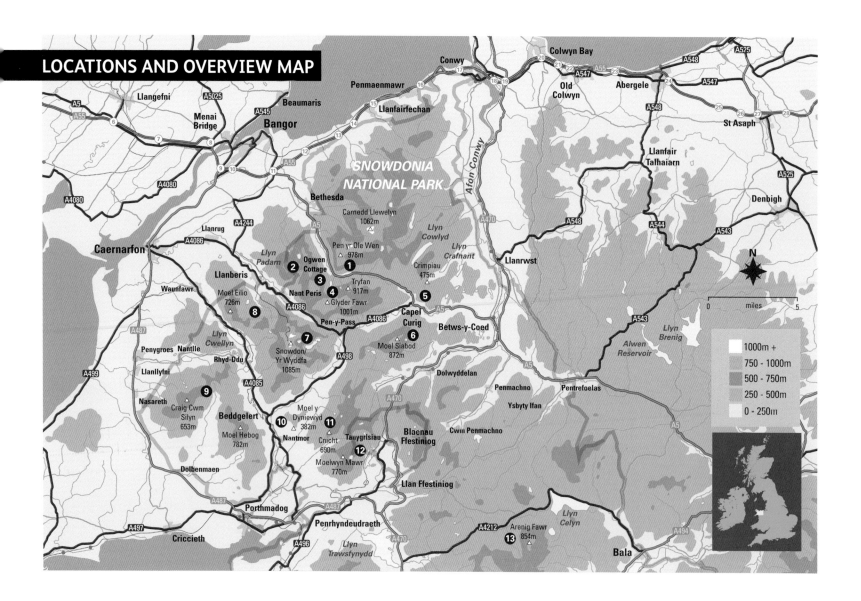

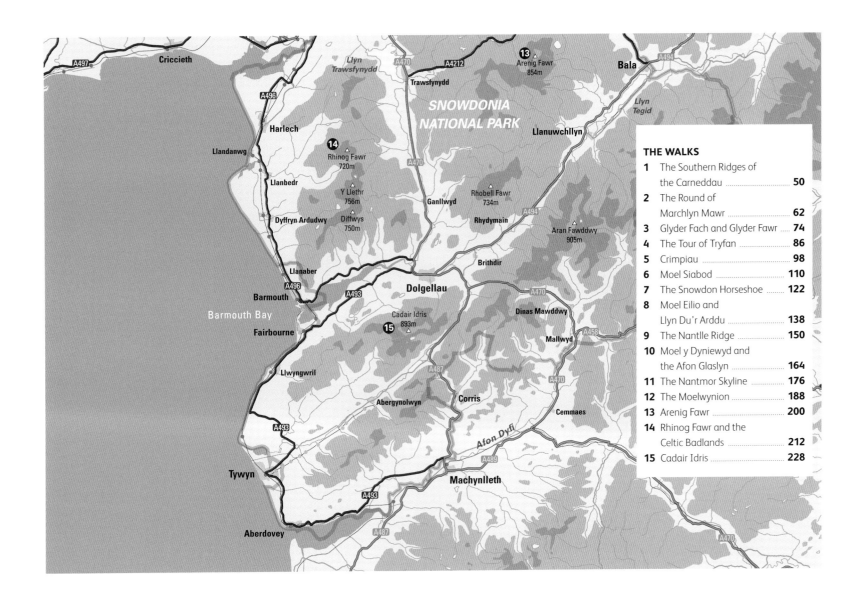

THE WALKS

The walks

Have you ever driven along the A5 and had your attention monopolised by Tryfan and the spectacular glacial cwms of the Glyderau? If so then you're not alone and with good reason. On the other side of the valley and rarely inspiring a second glance rise a range of whaleback lumps which couldn't be less interesting to those who seek something of the sublime to point their cameras at. Cinderella hills they may be but don't be deceived.

To the mountain photographer the Carneddau may appear to be a lost cause but they are built on a much grander scale than their Glyderau neighbours and don't give up their secrets so readily. If one is to get a taste of their true nature then roadside surveillance will not suffice, the Carneddau must be climbed.

This unique route presents a real challenge both physically, environmentally and photographically. On the approach march and walk out traditional studies are abundant but up on the plateau – which never falls below 3000ft – a dearth of small scale features necessitates a change of mindset. The ability to solve intricate compositional puzzles is a valuable one but will be of little help in this stony sub-arctic wasteland. Success will be found in casting aside your preconceptions and attuning yourself to a powerful landscape of epic proportions.

Previous spread: VP 2. Greg Knowles catching late light from Y Gribin. Four shot stitched panorama.
Canon 7D, 17-40mm at 19mm, ISO 100, 1/10 sec at f/11, tripod, 0.6 and 0.9 graduated filters.

VP 4. Looking South from Carnedd Llewelyn on an October afternoon.
Canon 6D, 24-70mm at 24mm, ISO 100, 1/100 sec at f/11,
1.5 graduated filter, tripod.

01 THE SOUTHERN RIDGES OF THE CARNEDDAU

The walk

From the lay-by cross the A5 and follow it towards Llyn Ogwen before turning right on a track which passes Glan Dena, the palatial home of the Midland Association of Mountaineers. Continue past the hut and pick up a path which crosses a stile. The path now becomes boggy and indistinct in places but a series of waymark stakes help guide the way.

Viewpoint 1 – Afon Lloer

Before long the Afon Lloer must be forded which can be achieved with care at a number of places along the way. The stream is a photographer's dream and a thorough examination is called for with its eastern bank offering the most potential. Compositions are dependent on water levels but there is always something to shoot with lone trees, waterfalls and the stunning view of Tryfan and the Ogwen Valley coming together to help create memorable landscape photographs.

VP 1. Tryfan and the Afon Lloer on a wet afternoon in June.
Canon 6D, 24-70mm at 24mm, ISO 100, 0.3 sec at f/16, polarising filter, 0.9 graduated filter, tripod graduated filter, tripod.

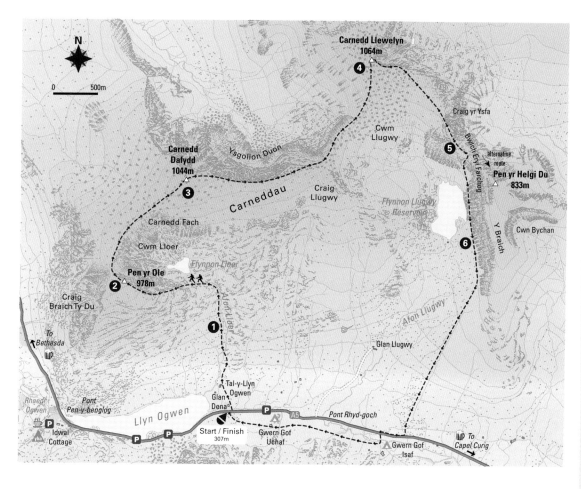

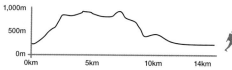

ELEVATION: Lowest: 307m   Highest: 1064m   Total ascent: 1000.5m
DISTANCE: 8.7 miles / 14 kilometres

How to get here

Park in the large lay-by on the south side of main A5 trunk road (adjacent to Gwern Gof Uchaf Campsite) which is accessed from the east (9 miles from Betws y Coed) or the north (five and a half miles from Bethesda).

Parking postcode: LL57 3LZ
Parking grid ref: SH 64887 60366
Parking lat/long: 53.123294, -4.0205627
Map: OS Explorer Map OL17 (1:25 000) Snowdon / Conwy Valley

Accessibility

This is a strenuous mountain walk of 8.7 miles / 14km and 1000 metres of ascent. After a period of wet weather the walk in to Cwm Lloer can be extremely boggy and gaiters are useful. In between Pen yr Ole Wen and Craig yr Ysfa the ground is stony and the main paths follow broad ridges where good navigation skills are essential in poor visibility. Two passages of easy scrambling – one taken in descent – require care. On the heights and away from the summit cairns shelter from the elements is scarce and the Carneddau are exposed to some of the worst weather imaginable. The summit of Carnedd Llewelyn is almost as far away as you can get from a road in Wales so in anything other than benign conditions this is a committing expedition not to be taken lightly.

Best time of year/day

The Afon Lloer is a wonderful sunrise location year-round and works well for sunsets in the spring and summer months. On the plateau late light is best with Carnedd Llewelyn being especially good from May to August. Changeable weather with racing clouds is worth pursuing in all four seasons with the Afon Lloer and Ffynnon Llugwy useful as standalone locations on doubtful days.

VP 2. Tryfan and the Glyderau from the upper reaches of Pen yr Ole Wen's south ridge on an April evening. Six shot stitched panorama.
Canon 7D, 17-40mm at 17mm, ISO 100, 1/15 sec at f/11, 0.6 graduated filter, tripod.

VP 3. Into the great unknown – Nick Matthews heading for Carnedd Llewelyn on a February afternoon. Canon 6D, 24-70mm at 32mm, ISO 100, 1/50 sec at f/11, 0.6 graduated filter.

Viewpoint 2 – Pen yr Ole Wen

Back on the western side of the stream continue up to a wall where a gate/stile gives access to the open mountain. A firm path develops following the stream and contours round to the left to enter Cwm Lloer, a wild glacial hollow hosting the triangular Ffynnon Lloer (spring of the moon). Carry on in a westerly direction towards an impregnable looking crag which guards the ridge above. By following a path of variable quality the foot of the ridge is met where a brief easy scramble up a well-worn gully spits you out on the ridge proper. 260 metres of stiff ascent leads to the barren summit of Pen yr Ole Wen which at first sight will appear to be an uninspiring photographic location. As is often the case a scout around is a good idea and on this occasion a foray to the top of the south ridge strikes gold. Tryfan and the Glyderau are seen to perfection rising above the Ogwen Valley 2000ft below. The further you descend the better the view becomes and thoughts of panoramic shots will no doubt come to mind when the full length of Llyn Ogwen is revealed. However, do remember that height lost must be won again and there is still work to do.

Viewpoint 3 – Carnedd Dafydd

From the summit cairn the way ahead hugs the edge of Cwm Lloer, descending slightly before a long steady climb to Carnedd Dafydd. Once past the ancient burial cairn of Carnedd Fach the view back towards Pen yr Ole Wen is immense with a phalanx of mighty peaks filling the horizon. Hereabouts the bleached stones of the path form a wonderful leading line. Dafydd's summit shelter is a good place to take a breather but is a difficult location to effectively photograph. The next section towards Bwlch Cyfryw Drum offers plenty of scope and a short descent southwards after 500 metres will bring Cwm Lloer back into view and is worth the extra effort involved if time is on your side. Staying with the main drag and to your left the 1000ft cliffs of Ysgolion Duon plunge into the profound depths of Cwm Llafar before arcing gracefully around to Carnedd Llewelyn. This beautiful curving skyline qualifies as one of the most enjoyable sections of ridge walking in Snowdonia and continues to the foot of Llewelyn's huge dome. It's time to get your head down and put in a bit of work to place the third highest peak in Wales under your boots.

Viewpoint 4 – Carnedd Llewelyn

The view south from Carnedd Llewelyn is one of extraordinary mountain grandeur but the seemingly featureless nature of this massive plateau will have you scratching your head as to how best to capture it. There are two very useful elements that can be included in your compositions to add foreground interest; the first is an old stone wall right in front of the shelter which snakes its way pleasingly into the scene and breaks up the monotony of an extensive hillside of scree and boulders. The second area of interest lies about 200 metres to the west where an interesting collection of rocky stooks provide innumerable possibilities and catch late light on spring and summer evenings.

Opposite left: VP 6. *Nick Matthews looking to Carnedd Llewelyn from Pen yr Helgi Du on a March afternoon. Canon 6D, 24-70mm at 24mm, ISO 100, 1/80 sec at f/11, polarising filter.* **Right**: VP 3. *The Ogwen Valley from above Cwm Lloer on an October evening. Canon 6D, 24-70mm at 24mm, ISO 100, 1/25 sec at f/11, 0.9 graduated filter, tripod.*

Bottom: VP 3. *The mountains of Northern Snowdonia from Carnedd Dafydd on an October afternoon. Four shot stitched panorama. Canon 6D, 24-70mm at 24mm, ISO 100, 1/40 sec at f/11, 0.9 graduated filter.*

Viewpoint 5 – Bwlch Eryl Farchog

The shelter is effectively the hub of four major ridges so on leaving the summit it is very important to locate the correct path which in this case trends in a south easterly direction. The going is stony at first but soon becomes an easy romp on grass before reaching the rocky outcrop at the top of Craig yr Ysfa which, along with Ysgolion Duon is one of the most formidable crags in Wales so watch your step if walking close to the edge. There then follows a short slabby scramble down onto the delectable ridge of Bwlch Eryl Farchog which can look intimidating from above but is relatively easy if taken steadily and with due care. Before you tackle the scramble spend a little time to consider the two peaks east of the Bwlch, Pen yr Helgi Du and Pen Lllithrig yr Wrach respectively which make great photographic subjects in moody conditions.

Viewpoint 6 – Ffynnon Llugwy

At the Bwlch you have two options, a steep clamber onto Pen yr Helgi Du (followed by a descent of Y Braich) where excellent retrospective views of your route can be enjoyed or down the zig zag path to Ffynnon Llugwy (my preference), a reservoir which somehow retains much of its wild appeal and in good light is wonderful to photograph with Llewelyn high and aloof beyond.

You'll no doubt be feeling it after such a big day and although the car is still a couple of miles away the walking couldn't be simpler. From the south side of Ffynnon Llugwy pick up the reservoir service road (with excellent views of Tryfan's east face) and follow it down the A5. Cross the road and turn right for about 250 metres and then left into Gwern Gof Isaf farm and campsite. After 100 metres turn right onto the old course of the A5 which in just over a mile takes you back to the lay-by where your chariot awaits.

VP 5. Dave Dear capturing a wintry Carnedd Llewelyn from Craig yr Ysfa in November. Canon 6D, 24-70mm at 24mm, ISO 100, 1/125 sec at f/8, polarising filter, 0.9 graduated filter.

Overleaf: *VP 4. Looking south on a May evening to the Snowdonian giants from Carnedd Llewelyn Four shot stitched panorama. Canon 7D. 17-40mm at 17mm, ISO 100, 1/4 sec at f/11, 0.9 graduated filter, tripod.*

02 THE ROUND OF MARCHLYN MAWR

On paper the horseshoe of ridges which cradle Marchlyn Mawr are an unattractive prospect for a photography walk. At the foot of Carnedd y Filiast is Penrhyn and on the south western flank of Elidir Fawr is Dinorwig which, in the late 19th century, were the two largest slate quarries in the world. Whole mountainsides were decimated; tiered galleries, gigantic holes and vast slate tips remain as a tribute to generations of Welshmen who worked in often appalling conditions for unscrupulous landowners. In 1974, to add further insult to Elidir's injuries, work began on the Dinorwig pumped storage scheme which disembowelled the mountain and irrevocably changed the nature of Llyn Peris and Marchlyn Mawr.

A rather disturbing picture you might think, but no amount of desolation can rob this walk of its inherent grandeur and potential for impressive mountain images. Lying at the northern and western margins of the Glyderau this walk feels out on a limb and enjoys an extensive coastal panorama along with unusual perspectives on Wales' highest mountains.

VP 1. Elidir Fawr and Marchlyn Mawr from Carnedd y Filiast on an April evening
Canon 6D, 24-70mm at 24mm, ISO 100, 1/50 sec at f/11.

02 THE ROUND OF MARCHLYN MAWR

The walk

From the end of the road, go through the kissing gate and follow the reservoir access road as it rises gently in twists and turns until a gate and stile signed for Carnedd y Filiast appear on the left. It's a scruffy start but things are about to get much better. Over the stile a vague path follows the fence line down to a steel footbridge which is crossed to reach another stile. A rising traverse then leads to a broad saddle and from here a steep pull on a shaley path followed by a tumble of boulders takes you to the summit shelter of Carnedd y Filiast, 'Cairn of the Greyhound Bitch'.

Viewpoint 1 – Carnedd y Filiast

Quite unexpectedly the view has grown enormously with the remainder of the day laid out before you. The summit area is a broad stony expanse capped with a cockscomb of rock suspended high above Marchlyn Mawr. The Carneddau giants lie across Nant Ffrancon and south the sweeping arc of Tryfan and the Glyderau demand your attention. This is a peak where conventional wide angle landscapes and tighter telephoto compositions both have their place. The onward route heads south to a stile right on the edge of Cwm Graianog where the Atlantic Slabs can be seen plunging 1000ft into the dark hollow below. Across the stile it's worth keeping to the left for intimate views of Nant Ffrancon until you reach the shelter on Mynydd Perfedd from which, in a south westerly direction, another stile finds you on the rim of Cwm Marchlyn.

VP 1. Tryfan from Carnedd y Filiast, March afternoon
Canon 7D, 17 – 40mm at 33mm, ISO 100, 1/160 sec at f/11.

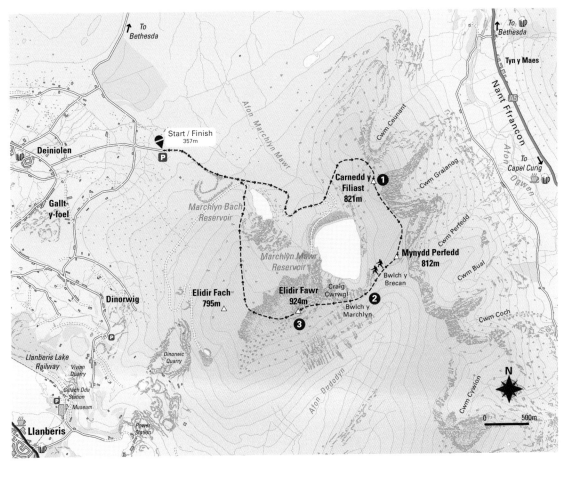

ELEVATION: Lowest: 357m   Highest: 924m   Total ascent: 630.4m

DISTANCE: 5.4 miles / 8.7 kilometres

How to get here

From Llanberis with Llyn Padarn on your right follow the A4086 out of the village and turn right onto the A4244 signed to Bangor. After 1.5 miles turn right onto the road signed to Deiniolen and Dinorwig. After about half-a-mile take a left signed to Marchlyn and a follow the road to the parking area at its end.

If traveling from Bethesda, head north west along the A5 and at the roundabout go left onto the A4244 passing through Felin Hen and Pentir. At the next roundabout go left and continue past the Texaco garage and take the first left which puts you and the Deiniolen/Dinorwig road mentioned above.

Parking postcode: LL55 3NA
Parking grid ref: SH 59677 63088
Parking lat/long: 53.146479, -4.099509
Map: OS Explorer Map OL17 (1:25 000 Snowdon/Conwy Valley)

Accessibility

This is a relatively undemanding walk of 5.5 miles / 8.7km with 630 metres of ascent. It does, however, traverse high mountains which require an ice axe and crampons in winter conditions.

Best time of year/day

In high summer a sunrise can work well on any of the summits but they really come into their own in the period just before and during sunset due to their westerly position. The very best time for photography on these mountains is during the winter months when snow lies on the tops and low angled light rakes across the landscape. In poor visibility competent navigation is needed to link the three summits and locate the descent from Elidir Fawr.

VP 1. The Carneddau giants from Carnedd y Filiast, April evening. Canon 6D, 24-70mm at 70mm, ISO 100, 1/200 sec at f/7.1.

Top left: VP 1. Tryfan and Foel Goch from Mynydd Perfedd on a March evening. Canon 6D, 24-70mm at 44mm, ISO 100, 1/10 sec at f/11, 0.6 graduated filter, tripod.

Above: VP 1. Looking over Caernarfon and the Menai Strait to the Wicklow Hills in Ireland – March. Canon 6D, 24-70mm at 28mm, ISO 100, 1.6 sec at f/11, 0.6 and 0.9 graduated filter, tripod.

VP 1. Karl Mortimer catching last light from Carnedd y Filliast – March. Canon 6D, 24-70mm at 28mm, ISO 100, 1.6 sec at f/11, 0.9 graduated filter, tripod.

Viewpoint 2 – After Mynydd Perfedd

The character of the terrain has suddenly changed; the broad grassy ridge has given way to a narrow arête punctuated with rocky towers which, while not difficult or too exposed, offers an easier path on its southern flank. Across the gulf of Cwm Dudodyn the Snowdon Massif thrusts skywards from the shadowy depths of the Llanberis Pass and Elidir Fawr rises ahead. It's a dramatic scene and one where, at the end of the day, the light can be very special; a grand spot for photographing fellow walkers in their natural habitat.

VP 3. Pen yr Ole Wen, Foel Goch and Tryfan February afternoon. Canon G12, 6.1mm, ISO 80, 1/640 sec at f/2.8, 0.9 graduated filter, tripod.

VP 1. A lone walker high on Elidir Fawr from Mynydd Perfedd January afternoon. Canon 6D, 24-70mm at 70mm, ISO 100, 1/250 sec at f/7.1.

VP 3. Moel Cynghorion and the Eifionydd hills from Elidir Fawr January evening. Canon 6D, 24-70mm at 70mm, ISO 100, 1/200 sec at f/8, 0.6 and 0.9 graduated filters, tripod.

02 THE ROUND OF MARCHLYN MAWR

Viewpoint 3 – Elidir Fawr

Before long the ridge broadens and after about 70 metres of ascent it levels off until a short clamber over boulders sees you onto Elidir Fawr's slender summit ridge. This is the high point of the day both literally and scenically boasting an astounding 360 degree view. All the high mountains of Snowdonia are visible along with the hills of the Lleyn and the Isle of Anglesey in its entirety as if seen from a plane. The summit ridge is relatively level for about 200 metres and all along its length reveals new insights into the valleys below. Take your time here to seek out the different facets of the view, employing different focal lengths whilst enjoying one of Snowdonia's most memorable mountain tops.

The descent route starts from a grassy hiatus in the ridge and trends in a north-westerly direction on a scree path until the plateau of Elidir Fach is underfoot. From here a northerly course veering slightly to the right where the ground begins to steepen will eventually see you back down to the reservoir access road and an easy return to the car.

Top: VP 3. Moel Eilio and Llyn Padarn from Elidir Fawr March afternoon.
Canon 7D, 17-40mm at 17mm, ISO 100, 1/160 sec at f/11, 0.9 graduated filter, tripod.

Bottom: VP 3. The peaks of the Ogwen Valley from Elidir Fawr – September.
Canon 6D, 24-70mm at 24mm, ISO 100, 1/80 sec at f/11, 0.6 graduated filter.

Overleaf: VP 3. Jamie Rooke enjoys the end of a perfect January day on Elidir Fawr. Six shot stitched panorama. *Canon 6D, 24-70mm at 24mm, ISO 100, 1/8 sec at f/11, 0.6 and 0.9 graduated filters, tripod.*

03 GLYDER FACH AND GLYDER FAWR

If there is one range above all others which epitomises the spirit of Snowdonia, then it is the Glyderau. For over a century hill goers have been enjoying adventurous days on these summits, crags and ridges. Before them, botanists and naturalists found much to study in cwms such as Idwal. These days, the scientists have gone but the walkers and climbers remain, joined by an increasing band of photographers, most of whom confine themselves to the lower regions of the Ogwen Valley where an abundance of photographic delights await.

Up on the heights – which culminate in Glyder Fach and Glyder Fawr, the latter breaching the 1000 metre contour – you'll find a barren plateau festooned with splinters of rock, spiky tors and a 'wind castle' fashioned by nature in gothic splendour. This is a stirring walk from start to finish where photogenic subjects, possibly dragons too, lurk around every corner and mountain grandeur is the order of the day. If that wasn't enough to chew on then this route throws in Y Garn, a bonus peak which completes this horseshoe walk around the Cwm Idwal skyline and a fine podium on which to end the day.

VP 1. Dan Aspel on Y Gribin on a beautiful March morning
Canon 6D, 24-70mm at 24mm, ISO 100, 1/8 sec
at f/11, tripod, 0.9 graduated filter.

03 GLYDER FACH AND GLYDER FAWR

The walk

From the Ogwen Cottage visitor centre the main Cwm Idwal path goes through a gate and crosses the bridge over a boisterous cascade before taking a less distinct left fork. Traverse boggy terrain – stepping stones facilitate a dry passage – to an excellent path which ascends steeply beside the Bochlwyd stream all the way up into Cwm Bochlwyd. The urge to tarry is strong but with much still to do why not come back on another day when you can give it the attention it deserves?

Viewpoint 1 – Y Gribin

On approaching the llyn a faint peaty trod develops and heads west before climbing a pitched path onto Y Gribin's broad back. The view across the cwm to Tryfan becomes more impressive with each successive rise until suddenly a small plateau known as the 'Football Pitch' is gained and the upper ramparts of the ridge are revealed to great effect. Two options now present themselves; a scrambly but easier path which takes a lower line on Y Gribin's the western flank or the grade one scramble of the ridge direct which involves a degree of exposure and rock handling but is the recommended route for the very best photographic possibilities. At several points along the ridge there are platforms which, with due care, can be paused upon to set up and photograph a dazzling landscape of lake and mountain.

Top: VP 1. An August evening on Y Gribin with Tryfan and the Carneddau beyond. Four shot stitched panorama. Canon 7D, 17-40mm at 17mm, ISO 100, 1/15 sec at f/11, tripod, 0.6 graduated filter.

Bottom: VP 3. Surveying Glyder Fawr's bleak moonscape on an atmospheric January afternoon. Canon 6D, 24-70mm at 24mm, ISO 100, 1/400 sec at f/11, tripod, 0.6 and 0.9 graduated filters.

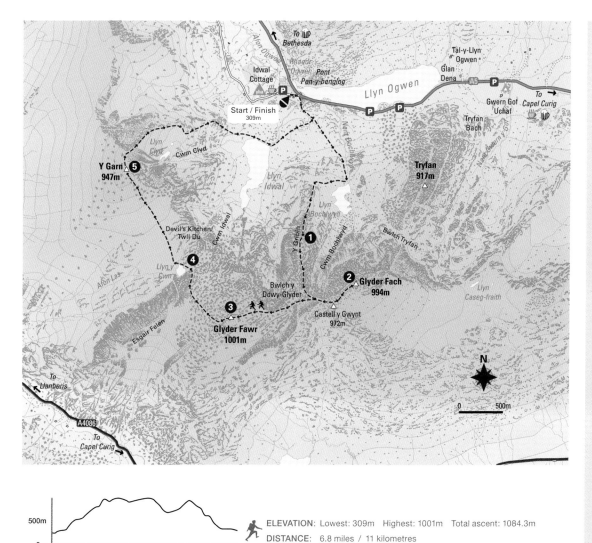

How to get here

Ogwen Cottage lies on the main A5 trunk road and be easily accessed from the east, 10 miles from Betws y Coed, or from the north, four and a half miles from Bethesda.

Parking postcode: LL57 3LZ
Parking grid ref: OS SH 64904 60412
Parking lat/long: 53.123294, -4.0205627
Map: OS Explorer Map OL17 (1:25 000) Snowdon / Conwy Valley

Accessibility

This is a strenuous high mountain walk of just under 7 miles / 11km with 1084 metres of ascent. The paths are generally good but on the Glyder plateau the stony nature of the ground makes paths vague and competent navigation skills are essential in poor visibility.

Best time of year/day

Glyder's Fach and Fawr catch the finest light at sunrise in the autumn and winter months and sunset in spring and summer and their tops are more often than not deserted at these times. Y Garn offers excellent golden hour light through all four seasons. Under winter conditions the character of this walk changes dramatically and becomes a serious outing that should not be attempted without an ice axe, crampons and experience in their use.

ELEVATION: Lowest: 309m   Highest: 1001m   Total ascent: 1084.3m
DISTANCE: 6.8 miles / 11 kilometres

03 GLYDER FACH AND GLYDER FAWR

Viewpoint 2 – Glyder Fach and Castell y Gwynt

At Bwlch y Ddwy Glyder the ridge gives up the ghost and hands can temporarily be put back into pockets. The logical continuation is to head straight for Glyder Fawr but with 'Fach' so close at hand a pilgrimage to this unique mountain top should be considered mandatory. By skirting the rim of Cwm Bochlwyd and contouring around Castell y Gwynt on its southern side Glyder Fach's chaos of rock features are there for the taking. The view southwards has opened up to reveal a tremendous panorama of southern Snowdonia ranging from Moel Siabod all the way to Cadair Idris almost 30 miles distant. This presents a good opportunity to experiment with longer focal lengths to isolate elements of the vast scene in front of you.

Take some time to investigate the many interesting outcrops (including the famous 'Cantilever') before heading back to the daddy of them all, Castell y Gwynt (Castle of the Wind in English) which lies about 150 metres south west of Glyder Fach's huge summit pile. Although this is one of the most prized photographic icons in Snowdonia, unique images can be made by repeated visits at different times of day. The difference in atmosphere at sunrise, midday and sunset can't be overstated.

VP 2. A golden November dawn on Glyder Fach. Two shot stitched panorama. Canon 6D, 24-70mm at 24mm, ISO 100, 1/5 sec at f/11, tripod, 0.9 graduated filter.

03 GLYDER FACH AND GLYDER FAWR

Viewpoint 3 – Glyder Fawr

The onward route returns to Bwlch y Ddwy Glyder before moving on to Glyder Fawr's bald dome, a place which, while not as immediately dramatic as 'Fach' is even more other-worldly with numerous rock formations littering an almost lunar landscape. Once again, it's worth scouting around to evaluate the compositional possibilities, many of which provide excellent foregrounds to the magnificent view of the Snowdon massif, the Llanberis lakes and the Irish Sea.

Viewpoint 4 – Llyn y Cwn

The initial descent from Glyder Fawr requires care in misty conditions but a line of cairns trending north west leads to a short-lived but eroded runnel of scree which in turn delivers you to the environs of Llyn y Cwn, a reedy lake and popular wild camping venue where late light is often excellent.

Top: VP 6. The harvest moon rises above Tryfan from Cwm Clyd, September. Canon 7D, 17-40mm at 17mm, ISO 100, 8 sec at f/11, 0.6 and 0.9 graduated filters.

Middle: VP 3. Looking east to Glyder Fach and Castell y Gwynt as the mist rolls in on a September evening. Canon 6d, 24-70mm at 70mm, ISO 100, 1/5 sec at f/11, tripod, 0.9 graduated filter.

Bottom: VP 3. Rock fingers on Glyder Fawr catching some late light on a June evening. Two shot stitched panorama. Canon 7D, 17-40mm at 17mm, ISO 160, 0.6 sec at f/13, tripod, 0.6 and 0.9 graduated filters.

VP 4. A March evening beside Llyn y Cwn. Canon 7D, 17-40mm at 17mm, ISO 100, 1/5 sec at f/11, tripod, 0.9 graduated filter.

03 GLYDER FACH AND GLYDER FAWR

Viewpoint 5 – Y Garn

Ahead lies Y Garn and if an 800ft slog is too much for you after the rigours of the day then a path which heads north east through a rubble filled slot will take you to the Devils Kitchen path and an escape to Cwm Idwal. It would be a real shame though to miss out on this final 3000ft peak from which an extraordinary view revealing the entire route can be savoured. For year-round late light the summit of Y Garn is the finest vantage point in the Ogwen mountains so make the most of it before returning to the shadowed depths of the valley! From the summit cairn follow the edge of Cwm Clyd (beware of cornices in winter) roughly north for 150 metres until an obvious shaley path leads down to the delightful north east ridge eventually reaching Cwm Clyd where two small llyns and their attendant pools are worth spending some time with if times allows. A steep pitched path then takes you down into Cwm Idwal where the lakeside path can be followed easily back to your starting point.

VP 5. Dark Clouds gathering over Llyn Ogwen and Llyn Idwal from the summit of Y Garn, October evening. Canon 6D, 24-70mm at 24mm, ISO 100, 1/6 sec at f/11, tripod, 0.9 graduated filter

Next spread: *VP 2. Southern Snowdonia from Glyder Fach on a hazy November Morning. Canon 6D, 24-70mm at 70mm, ISO 100, 1/400 sec at f/8.*

VP 5. The Ogwen mountains from Y Garn on an April evening. Eight shot stitched panorama. Canon 7D, 17-40mm at 17mm, ISO 100, 1/15 sec at f/11, tripod, 0.9 graduated filter.

04 THE TOUR OF TRYFAN

The mountains of Snowdonia come in many shapes and sizes but none are as distinctive or arresting as the mighty Tryfan. A bristling peak which fires the imagination and throws down an irresistible challenge to all ambitious walkers, Tryfan is wonderful to look at but even better to climb. The seemingly inaccessible summit is buttressed on all sides by steep rock and furnished with twin pillars – known since time immemorial as Adam and Eve – which are often mistaken for people by passing motorists. To stand beside them or even leap from one to the other is a rite of passage and usually accomplished via the classic north ridge scramble, a daunting prospect for some perhaps. There is, however, an easier way within the powers of sure-footed photographers which scores highly in terms of awe-inspiring scenery and fits neatly into an itinerary which circumnavigates the mountain and studies her from every angle.

This is a mountain photography walk straight out of the top drawer with an abundance of subjects to point your camera at. During this 'tour of Tryfan' you'll walk grassy ridges, find peaty pools and visit a fine outlying summit before meeting Adam and Eve for a thrilling shoot at over 3000 feet. The outward leg isn't short of photographic bounty either in the form of Cwm Bochlwyd, a grand glacial hollow with its stunning lake. What are you waiting for?

VP 1. Glyder Fach and Tryfan from Braich y Ddeugwm on an October afternoon. Canon 6D, 24-70mm at 24mm, ISO 100, 1/100 sec at f/8, 0.9 graduated filter, tripod.

04 THE TOUR OF TRYFAN

The walk

From the car park at Gwern Gof Isaf farm and campsite walk towards the farmhouse (where you should pay for parking) to the right of which a step stile is crossed and then another a short distance beyond a tumbledown wall which leads to the start of Braich y Ddeugwm (arm of the two hollows).

Viewpoint 1 – Braich y Ddeugwm Ridge

A faint path follows the left hand side of the ridge but gaining the crest as soon as possible is a fast track to a staggering scene of mountain dominance. Across the heathery expanse of Cwm Tryfan Bristly Ridge and Tryfan's soaring buttresses are seen in all their glory. The ridge rises steadily through rock outcrops and passes large peaty puddles affording myriad compositions until an extensive moorland plateau is underfoot.

VP 2. A Brocken Spectre on Y Foel Goch.
Canon 7D, 17-40mm at 40mm, ISO 100, 1/60 sec at f/11.

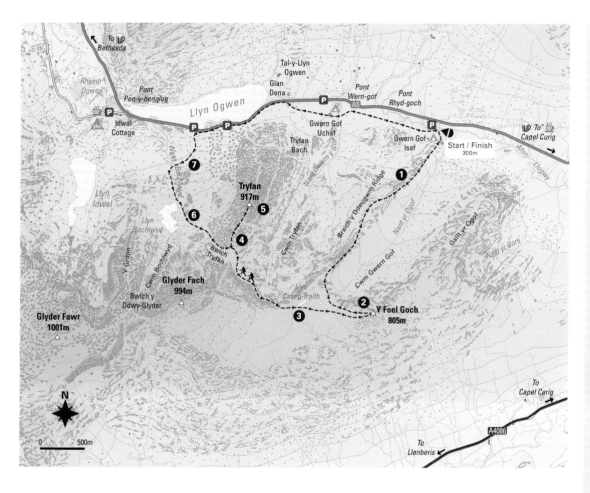

How to get here

Gwern Gof Isaf campsite lies on the main A5 trunk road and be easily accessed from the east – 7.5 miles from Betws y Coed – or the north, 7 miles from Bethesda.

Parking postcode: LL24 0EU
Parking grid ref: OS SH 66834 60518
Parking lat/long: 53.122225, -3.966162
Map: OS Explorer Map OL17 (1:25 000) Snowdon / Conwy Valley

Accessibility

This is a moderately strenuous high mountain walk of just under 7 miles / 11km with 800 metres of ascent. The paths are generally good but the area around Llyn y Caseg Fraith can be very boggy in all but prolonged periods of dry weather so gaiters are a useful addition to your kit. The ascent of Tryfan's South Ridge involves sections of very easy scrambling.

Best time of year/day

Braich y Ddeugwm, Llyn y Caseg Fraith and Y Foel Goch are wonderful year-round sunrise locations and usually very quiet while Tryfan and Cwm Bochlwyd are great for late light in the summer months. Under winter conditions Tryfan becomes a potentially serious climb that should not be attempted without an ice axe, crampons and experience in their use.

ELEVATION: Lowest: 300m   Highest: 917m   Total ascent: 769.6m
DISTANCE: 6.8 miles / 11 kilometres

VP 2. Gallt yr Ogof and the eastern Carneddau from Y Foel Goch on a chilly November evening. Fuji X-T10, 16-55mm at 18mm, ISO 200, 1/60 sec at f/11.

04 THE TOUR OF TRYFAN

Viewpoint 2 – Y Foel Goch

Once the plateau has been reached a great opportunity arises for a short detour onto Y Foel Goch, a seldom trodden peak with astonishing views. A leftward trending ascent around the head of Cwm Gwern Gof will soon see you sitting by the cairn where rocks and a shallow pool provide foreground interest to an expansive northern vista. This really is a great place to be and one to which you will want to return time and again.

Viewpoint 3 – Llyn y Caseg Fraith

From Y Foel Goch walk in a westerly direction until you can see a group of small pools on the plateau below. Head across boggy terrain to reach them and enjoy one of the most enchanting locations in the Welsh mountains. Llyn y Caseg Fraith is the largest of the pools and on still days Tryfan is reflected on its dark waters, a scene that is highly prized and sought after by every Snowdonian mountain photographer but don't let that be the end of your endeavours. Scout around and check out the other pools and rocky outcrops or, for something a little bit radical, try omitting Tryfan from the image altogether. This is also a prime wild camp site for sunrise seekers with an aversion for walking up in the dark.

Top: *VP 2. Fleeting light on Tryfan's East Face from Y Foel Goch – September afternoon. Canon 6D, 24-70mm at 28mm, ISO 100, 1/10 sec at f/11, polarising filter, 0.9 graduated filter, tripod.*
Bottom: *VP 2. A hazy March afternoon on Y Foel Goch. Canon 6D, 24-70mm at 24mm, ISO 100, 1/20 sec at f/11, 0.9 graduated filter, tripod.*

Overleaf: *VP 3. Glyder Fawr engulfed by September morning mist from Llyn y Caseg Fraith. Canon 6D, 24-70mm at 24mm, ISO 100, 1/25 sec at f/8, 0.6 and 0.9 graduated filters, tripod.*

Viewpoint 4 – Bwlch Tryfan

Two hundred metres west of Llyn y Caseg Fraith a path on the right dips down slightly before contouring across the head of Cwm Tryfan on the way to Bwlch Tryfan. The bwlch sits between Bristly Ridge and Tryfan's South Ridge and as a natural pass it can be a blowy place as the wind tends to funnel through the gap gaining strength as it goes. This is a good place to take stock and ready yourself for the climax of the day. A dry stone wall with several stiles along its length provides shelter from the wind but also doubles as a brilliant compositional device forming a strong leading line towards the now pyramidal Tryfan, your next destination.

Viewpoint 5 – Tryfan

From the Bwlch Tryfan head NW keeping the wall to your right a pick up a path that leads directly towards Tryfan's South Ridge. The ascent is rough going and the occasional use of hands is needed but nowhere is the scrambling sustained or exposed unless more difficult variations are sought out. If it doesn't look like thousands of others have trodden the ground beneath your feet you are off route! Before long you will reach the South Peak and across a deep gully Adam and Eve come into view. A slight descent and a short climb are all that separates you from Tryfan's central and highest summit. The view is marvellous through 360 degrees and the situation exciting in the extreme.

Unless it's dawn or dusk you are unlikely to have the place to yourself but that isn't necessarily a bad thing as figures in the landscape work very well here, adding scale to the epic nature of the surroundings. Catching people on the north and south peaks can lend drama and human interest to your images while shooting 'the leap' from Adam to Eve (and back again) is a must do. To grab the shot a fast shutter speed is needed and continuous shooting mode on your camera helps too. Remember to be courteous and ask the 'leaper' if they mind you taking their photograph. Getting their email address and promising to share the photograph goes a long way to securing the shot in my experience.

Top left: VP 4. Tryfan's South Ridge brooding above the bwlch.
Canon 6D, 24-70mm at 28mm, ISO 100, 1/50 sec at f/11, 0.9 graduated filter, tripod.

Top right: VP 5. The time honoured tradition – a climber jumps from Eve to Adam.
Canon 7D, 17-40mm at 17mm, ISO 320, 1/640 sec at f/7.1.

Left: VP 5. Dave Dear on his way to the summit of Tryfan late on a June afternoon.
Canon 6D, 24-70mm at 26mm, ISO 100, 1/50 sec at f/11, 0.9 graduated filters.

04 THE TOUR OF TRYFAN

Viewpoint 6 – Cwm Bochlwyd

Retrace your steps carefully back to Bwlch Tryfan and follow the path NW into Cwm Bochlwyd. Llyn Bochlwyd soon appears below and in shape resembles the outline of Australia. Not far above or below the path good vantage points can be found from which to shoot the lake in the context of its high cwm setting. Lower down it is possible to walk around the lake which is boggy in places but if time is on your side it can be a rewarding exercise to explore the many compositions available by the water's edge and on the various mounds and moraines.

Viewpoint 7 – Bochlwyd Stream

At the outflow of the llyn, cross the stream and follow it down to a steep pitched path. Where the path starts to level out turn right and cross the stream again under the climbing crag of Bochlwyd Buttress. An intermittent marshy path heads across country with great views of Tryfan's West Face and North Ridge. This is a grand spot for utilising a longer lens and picking out silhouetted figures scrambling high on the mountain. Eventually the path arrives at a parking area where a short spell of road walking along the A5 leads to a gate just beyond Llyn Ogwen and the foot of Tryfan's North Ridge. A path now follows the route of the old A5 taking you back to the start of the walk. En route it is worth a detour to Tryfan Bach – large slab of rock – where novice climbers will almost certainly be seen being put through their paces- and a wonderful place to halt and consider a memorable photographic journey.

VP 6. Looking across Llyn Bochlwyd to the Nant Ffrancon on a blustery October afternoon. Canon 6D, 24-70mm at 24mm, ISO 100, 1/80 sec at f/7.1, 0.9 graduated filter, tripod.

***Opposite**: VP 7. High on Tryfan's North Ridge, May afternoon. Canon 6D, 70-300mm at 300mm, ISO 400, 1/1250 sec at f/7.1.*

I've often said that it's better to be on an ugly mountain looking at a beautiful one than vice versa and Crimpiau is a perfect case in point. Falling short of 'official' mountain status by 450ft and being little more than a minor incident on a long knobbly ridge bound for Creigiau Gleision, lowly Crimpiau harbours a secret that few would suspect from below, and that is the biggest 'bang for buck' view in Snowdonia National Park; a mini mountain then, but one with an unmatched vista of Wales' three highest ranges.

On this walk you're never more than 2km away from the nearest road, yet once the creature comforts of Capel Curig's pubs and cafes are left behind it assumes an air of remoteness quite at odds with its accessible nature. This makes for a great route if you need to indulge in some proper mountain photography but haven't the time (or energy) for a big day on the high tops.

VP 4. Capel Curig, Dyffryn Mymbyr and the surrounding mountains from Clogwyn Mawr. Two shot stitched panorama Canon 6D, 24-70mm at 24mm, ISO 100, 0.4sec at f/11, 0.6 and 0.9 graduated filters, tripod.

05 CRIMPIAU

The walk

From the car park, walk up the lane past Joe Brown's and the Pinnacle Stores before (carefully) crossing the A5. Go over the stile beside St Curig's Church and follow the path to a break in the wall.

Viewpoint 1 – Y Pincin/The Pinnacles

To your right are the distinctive Capel Curig Pinnacles (marked Y Pincin on the map) which you should definitely take the time to visit. A short detour and some very easy scrambling on their south side gives access to several rocky platforms. This location is a good first taste of the western view which will feature prominently throughout the day and the temptation to linger is strong but must be resisted; the best is yet to come.

Looking down the Ogwen Valley on a February afternoon.
Canon 6D, 24-70mm at 24mm, ISO 100, 1/640 at f/8,
0.9 graduated filter.

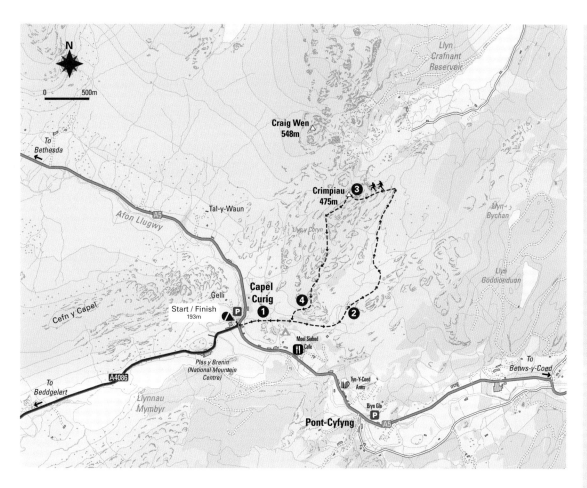

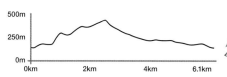

ELEVATION: Lowest: 193m   Highest: 475m   Total ascent: 367.8m

DISTANCE: 4 miles / 3.7 kilometres

How to get here

The car park is behind Pinnacle Stores in Capel Curig on the A4086 just off the main A5 trunk road and is easily accessed from the east (5.5 miles from Betws y Coed) and from the north (10 miles from Bethesda).

Parking postcode: LL24 0EN
Parking grid ref: SH 72052 58244
Parking lat/long: 53.105103, -3.912425
Map: OS Explorer Map OL17 (1:25 000) Snowdon/Conwy Valley

Accessibility

This is an easy hill walk of just under 4 miles / 3.7km with 370 metres of ascent. The paths are generally well trodden and easy to follow if a little boggy in places on the Crimpiau/Clogwyn Mawr ridge. Under snow the short steep descent from Clogwyn Mawr requires care to avoid a slip but being relatively low lying the route is rarely adversely affected by winter conditions.

Best time of year/day

To get the best photographically from this route it should be done in the morning and this applies to all four seasons. Dawn is especially rewarding from Crimpiau but for an easier start to the day or a quick fix Clogwyn Mawr can be reached in around 30 minutes from the car park.

VP 1. An incoming storm over Dyffryn Mymbyr from the Capel Curig pinnacles – August afternoon. Canon 7D, 17-40mm at 17mm, ISO 100, 1/125sec at f/8, tripod.

VP 2. Moel Siabod and Bryn Tyrch Farm – June morning. Canon 7D, 17-40mm at 17mm, ISO 100, 1/50sec at f/11, 0.9 graduated filter.

05 CRIMPIAU

Viewpoint 2 – Nant y Geuallt

Return to the path and follow it to another stile, over which you'll pass through enchanting broad-leaved woodland before emerging above Bryn Tyrch Farm and Plas Curig Youth Hostel. A halt here will reveal an expanded view and a good opportunity to photograph the farm and hostel in the true context of their mountain setting.

Onwards (ignoring twin stiles) you'll begin to feel a change. Cross the footbridge, take the left hand branch of the path and enter a wild and woolly valley. You're now in Nant y Geuallt, a secretive land of shaggy hills and humpy moraine. It's an area where few tread and even fewer spend time with their cameras. With a little investigation of the various nooks and crannies unusual images of Moel Siabod and the Snowdon Range are there for the taking.

Viewpoint 3 – Crimpiau

The path now blazes a trail into the heart of the valley, rising gradually as it goes to a narrow pass which drops down to Llyn Crafnant. From a flat grassy area at the top of the pass a left fork climbs steadily up Crimpiau's eastern flank until a brief clamber over boulders puts you slap bang on the summit.

This is a moment you won't forget in a hurry and after the meagre effort of the walk in you are confronted with an incredible scene worthy of a much higher mountain top. Tryfan and the Glyderau take centre stage, bisecting the valleys of Mymbyr and Ogwen with Siabod and the Carneddau acting as book-ends. Instinct will no doubt lead you – quite rightly – to shooting a panorama but it's also well worth using a zoom to get in closer to various elements for simplified compositions.

As good as the westward view undoubtedly is, don't neglect to look behind you, where the full length of Llyn Crafnant can also be enjoyed. If that wasn't enough to be thinking about, Carneddau ponies are often to be seen on and around Crimpiau; if you are lucky they might be there to add something a little bit special to your photographs.

*Top: VP 3. Moel Siabod and the Snowdon Range from Nant y Geuallt – August dawn.
Canon 7D, 17-40mm at 17mm, ISO 100, 1/4sec at f/11, 0.9 graduated filter, tripod.*

Bottom: *Dawn over Llyn Crafnant from Crimpiau – November.
Canon 7D, 17-40mm at 17mm, ISO 100, 0.3sec at f/11, 0.9 graduated filter, tripod.*

VP 3. Carneddau pony on Crimpiau – November afternoon. Canon 7D, 17-40mm at 28mm, ISO 250, 1/125 at f/11.

VP 3. Early morning light from Crimpiau – August. Two shot stitched panorama. Canon 7D, 17-40mm at 17mm, ISO 100, 1/15sec at f/8, 0.9 graduated filter, tripod.

05 CRIMPIAU

Viewpoint 4 – Clogwyn Mawr

The outward route is a splendid ridge walk weaving through patches of bog, a maze of rocky knolls and passing tiny Llyn y Coryn on the way. There are various ways to go but eventually the ridge gives up the ghost with one final belvedere to be visited, Clogwyn Mawr.

Once again it's all about the western prospect but this time, as on the pinnacles, Dyffryn Mymbyr with its twin lakes, Moel Siabod and the distant Snowdon Range are the main points of interest. This is a grand vantage point best experienced early on an autumnal morning when mist fills the valley below. From Clogwyn Mawr descend the way you came and cross a stile closely followed by another where a steep grassy path leads down into the woodland from earlier in the day. Retrace your steps back to the car park with a memory card full of images and a desire to return to Crimpiau as soon as possible.

VP 4. Morning mist over Capel Curig – September.
Canon 7D, 17-40mm at 40mm, ISO 100, 1/25sec at f/8, tripod.

06 MOEL SIABOD

For those approaching Snowdonia from the east, Moel Siabod's shapely profile is a compelling sight and a sure sign that the foothills have been left behind; mountain country awaits. Staunchly independent, Siabod has one of the largest footprints of a single hill in Europe and by falling short of the 3000ft contour by 140 feet it sees fewer visitors than its higher neighbours. In days gone by it played host to local quarrymen and bears scars which are slowly being reclaimed by nature.

Evan Roberts was one of the many who toiled in the quarries and after coming across purple saxifrage on the mountain he embarked on an odyssey of self-education which ultimately saw him become a respected authority on alpine flora and the first warden of the Cwm Idwal National Nature Reserve in 1953.

For a mountain photography walk Siabod is a fine objective. Ramshackle quarry buildings and their attendant pools provide a link to its industrial heritage while a remote cwm, two airy ridges and a peerless view from the summit combine to ensure a day full of adventure, exploration and great photography.

VP 6. Winter dawn – Moel Siabod. Four shot stitched panorama
Canon 6D, 24-70mm at 24mm, ISO 100, 1/20 sec at f/11, 0.6
graduated filter, tripod.

06 MOEL SIABOD

The walk

From the car park at Bryn Glo cross the A5 and turn right where, after 50 metres Cyfyng Falls can be seen flowing beneath the old stone bridge (Pont Cyfyng), a picturesque scene which becomes very impressive when the Afon Llugwy is in spate.

Go over the bridge and take the second of two footpaths where a cattle grid is crossed to follow a steep tree-lined tarmac track which leads via a signed diversion to a stile beside the Siabod holiday cottages.

Viewpoint 1
Beyond the stile an old cart track is gained and after a short rise Moel Siabod bursts into view across its bleak moorland setting.

Viewpoint 2
The track continues over two more stiles giving easy walking and distant views of the Glyderau and Carneddau before arriving at an unnamed lake. This is a great place to stop and the feeling hereabouts is one of the mountain finally welcoming you into its company.

VP 1. Pont Cyfyng – October
Canon 6D, 24-70mm at 47mm, ISO 100,
1/5 sec at f/18, polarising filter, tripod.

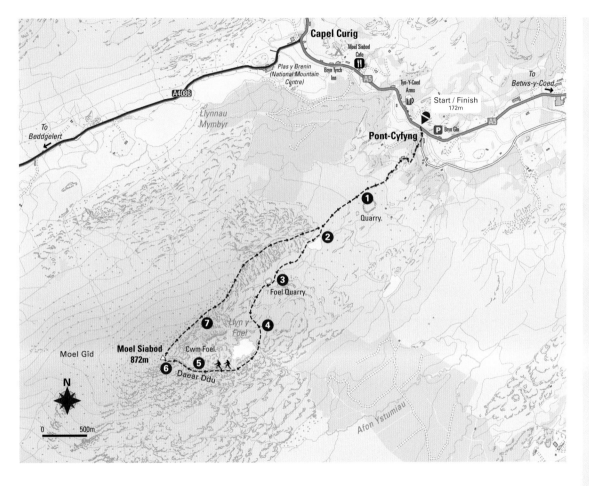

How to get here

The car park at Bryn Glo is in Capel Curig on the main A5 trunk road and is easily accessed from the east, 4.5 miles from Betws y Coed, and from the north, 11 miles from Bethesda.

Parking postcode: LL24 0DT
Parking grid ref: SH 73594 57093
Parking lat/long: 53.096044, -3.889208
Map: OS Landranger Map 115 (1:50 000) Snowdon/Yr Wyddfa

Accessibility

This is a moderately difficult mountain walk of 5.7 miles /9.3km and 770 metres of ascent. The path into Cwm Foel is excellent but the cwm can be boggy so gaiters are a useful addition to your kit. There is avoidable easy scrambling on the Daear Ddu and north east ridges but the rock can become greasy in wet weather. There are no paths on Moel Siabod's summit plateau and competent navigation skills are essential to locate the north east ridge in poor visibility.

Best time of year/day

Cwm Foel and Daear Ddu catch good morning and sunrise light all throughout the year. The summit and north east ridge are great for year round sunrises and sunsets. Siabod is a hill for all seasons though in winter conditions an ice axe, crampons and experience in their use should be considered essential if the full route is followed.

ELEVATION: Lowest: 172m Highest: 872m Total ascent: 771.9m
DISTANCE: 5.7 miles / 9.3 kilometres

06 MOEL SIABOD

Viewpoint 3 – Foel Quarry

Onwards and the path gets rougher, rounding an old spoil heap as it goes before reaching Foel Quarry. Here you'll find lots of old buildings in various states of dilapidation to explore and the quarry itself which is an enchanting pool hemmed in by steep walls of slate.

Viewpoint 4 – Llyn y Foel

Passing left of the quarry pool the path strikes upwards into a wilder landscape where, apart from the path itself, there are no signs of man's intervention. After a brief ascent and quite unexpectedly, Cwm Foel is revealed in all its glory. To the right is the towering headwall with crags cleaved by deep gullies, straight ahead raking from left to right is the Daear Ddu ridge (your route to the summit) and below is Llyn y Foel, a gorgeous glacial lake replete with two small islands set magnificently in a heathery bowl. This is a place where you'll want to linger and one which calls for a thorough investigation. The lake shore and an area of pools and rocky bluffs 500 metres due east of the main path are good places to start.

Viewpoint 5 – Daear Ddu

A faint peaty path through heather and rock passes to the left of the lake and leads to the foot of the Daear Ddu (Black Earth) ridge which is much easier than it looks from below. Clamber over boulders onto the crest and pick your way up the broad ridge with your surroundings becoming increasingly more spectacular. Nowhere is the ascent committing and there is always an easy alternative on the left hand side if a step appears too hard. At regular intervals there are large platforms from which to admire the view and compose your photographs. Having a friend to pose for you can be a very effective device for adding a sense scale to your shots.

VP 4. Dawn in Cwm Foel January. Six shot stitched panorama.
Canon 7D, 17-40mm at 17mm, ISO 100, 1/5 sec at f/11, 0.9 graduated filter, tripod.

VP 3. The Pool at Foel Quarry April morning. Canon 6D, 24-70mm at 24mm, ISO 100, 1/50sec at f/11, circular polarising filter.

VP 6. The Snowdon Horseshoe – pre dawn from Moel Siabod. Canon 6D, 24-70mm at 24mm, ISO 100 1/8 sec at f/11, 0.6 graduated filter, tripod.

VP 6. Snowdon and Moel Hebog from Moel Siabod October afternoon. Canon 7D, 17-40mm at 17mm, ISO 100, 1/125 sec at f/8, tripod, 0.6 and 0.9 graduated filters.

06 MOEL SIABOD

Viewpoint 6 – Moel Siabod summit

After a brief hiatus at half height the ridge gathers itself once more until, at the very last minute, the trig point comes into view. Siabod's summit is surprisingly broad but its isolated nature means that the view is incredible in both its extent and beauty. There are shots to be had through 360 degrees and of an evening, if you are lucky, dazzling shows of crepuscular rays can be enjoyed. I've experienced this phenomenon more times on Siabod than on any other mountain in Snowdonia.

Viewpoint 7 – North East Ridge

When you've managed to tear yourself away from the summit the way down starts along the north east ridge which forms a prominent rocky arm high above Cwm Foel. The ridge is less hands on than Daear Ddu but is very entertaining and extremely photogenic; it's a great place to be. Slabs and boulders offer foregrounds to a terrific retrospective view of your ascent route but longer focal lengths are also worth working with to frame tighter compositions of the surrounding hills. The ridge eventually loses momentum and turns to grass where a path can be picked up and followed easily down to the cart track and a simple stroll retracing your steps back to Capel Curig.

Top: VP 6. Glyder Fach, Tryfan and the Carneddau November afternoon. Canon 7D, 17-40mm at 33mm, ISO 100, 1/40 sec at f/11, tripod, 0.9 graduated filter.

Bottom: VP 6. A blaze of glory on Siabod's summit November evening. Canon 7D, 17-40mm at 17mm, ISO 100, 1.5 sec at f/15, 0.6 and 0.9 graduated filters, tripod.

Next spread: VP 5. Kevin O'brian high above Llyn y Foel on a September afternoon. Four shot stitched panorama. Canon 7D, 17-40mm at 17mm, ISO 100, 1/60 sec at f/11.

VP 7. Pre-dawn on Moel Siabod's north east ridge December. Canon 7D, 17-40mm at 17mm, ISO 100, 0.8 sec at f/11, tripod.

07 THE SNOWDON HORSESHOE

It has long been fashionable to knock Snowdon with its engineered paths, railway and summit café. Add to that the hundreds of thousands of visitors per year – Snowdon is said to be the busiest mountain in the world – with the resulting noise and litter and you've a recipe that may not be to everyone's taste. That, however, is just one side of the coin, the other being a mountain massif which is rich in history and folklore, architecturally complex and undeniably beautiful with a grandeur unmatched anywhere south of the border. To experience the magic of Snowdon you must go early or late in the day which, as luck would have it, are the times that landscape photographers love the most.

There are six main paths up onto Yr Wyddfa (Snowdon's summit) which can be followed by any able bodied person. Away from those the classic itinerary and one of the finest expeditions in the British Isles is the Snowdon Horseshoe which has few peers in terms of mountain scenery and photographic potential. While this isn't the longest route in the book it is technically, physically and mentally the most demanding, involving an exposed ridge traverse and sections of grade 1 scrambling. With the right amount of experience this is an incredibly rewarding day out and should be high on the list of every ambitious mountain photographer.

VP 2. Lara Turner on the Crib Goch Pinnacles – July evening. Four Shot Stitched Panorama. Canon 6D, 24-70mm at 24mm, ISO 100, 1.3 sec at f/11, 0.6 graduated filter, tripod.

The walk

Most folk begin the walk by taking the Pyg Track as far as Bwlch y Moch but for photographers and connoisseurs there is a much finer way to start the day. From the car park at Pen y Pass follow the Miner's Track for about 200 metres until a faint path (easily missed) doubles back sharply up the hillside on your right. Follow this through various twists and turns until you arrive at a shallow col and a step-stile.

Viewpoint 1 – The Horns

You are now on 'The Horns', a curving ridge of hummocks, small pools and rock outcrops which provides fine views of Llyn Llydaw and the peaks of the horseshoe on one side with the Llanberis Pass on the other. Take time to walk around and scope out the many possibilities for unique shots; not many come this way. The onward route keeps the fence on your left and negotiates a few ups and downs before descending to Bwlch y Moch. Here the path divides; left for the Pyg Track, right to Pen y Pass and straight ahead for Crib Goch which looms above, your next port of call.

How to get here

Pen y Pass is on the A4086 5 miles from Capel Curig and 5 miles from Llanberis. From Capel Curig leave the A5 at the junction of the A4086 (Pinnacle Pursuits general store on the corner) and follow the road before turning right just after the Pen y Gwryd Hotel. From Llanberis simply drive up the A4086 to Pen y Pass.

Parking postcode: LL55 4NY
Parking grid ref: SH 64737 55628
Parking lat/long: 53.080960, -4.020820
Map: OS Explorer Map OL17 (1:25 000)
Snowdon / Conwy Valley

Accessibility

This is a stupendous high mountain traverse of 7.4 miles / 12km with 1245 metres of ascent and is only suitable for experienced mountain walkers with a head for heights. The terrain varies from faint, boggy tracks on The Horns to very exposed scrambling on Crib Goch and everything inbetween. The way is well trodden throughout but in poor visibility special attention should be paid to locate the descents to Bwlch y Saethau and Cwm Dyli which are marked with a fingerstone and cairn respectively.

Car parking at Pen y Pass can be problematic during the summer and bank holidays when it is wise to arrive by 7am at the very latest. Alternative parking can be found either side of the Pen y Gwryd Hotel or in Nant Peris where a large park and ride scheme is in operation (check the Snowdon Sherpa online timetables for seasonal variations).

VP 2. Looking down Dyffryn Mymbyr to Moel Siabod and Capel Curig during a November pre-dawn. Canon 6D, 24-70mm at 38mm, ISO 100, 0.4 sec at f/7.1, 0.6 – 0.9 graduated filters, tripod.

Opposite: VP 1. Moel Siabod from The Horns on a February morning. Canon 6D, 24-70mm at 24mm, ISO 100, 1/40 sec at f/11, polarising filter, 0.9 graduated filter, tripod.

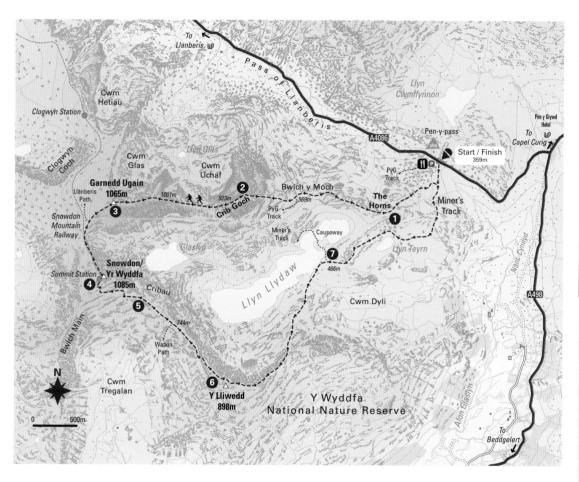

Best time of year/day

The Snowdon Horseshoe is a route for all seasons but when under snow and ice it becomes a serious mountaineering expedition and should only be attempted by those experienced in graded winter climbing. Sunrise shoots are especially profitable from The Horns, Llyn Llydaw and Crib Goch where, if ascending in the pre-dawn, prior knowledge of the route is advised. Snowdon's summit is unbearably crowded at weekends, bank holidays and weekdays during the summer months but is usually much quieter during the hour approaching sunset and preceding sunrise when, it's not unheard of to find yourself up there alone which is an experience well worth pursuing.

ELEVATION: Lowest: 359m   Highest: 1085m   Total ascent: 1245.1m

DISTANCE: 7.4 miles / 12 kilometres

Viewpoint 2 – Crib Goch

A good path leads over a stile before scrambling up easy slabs and scree until your way is barred by an intimidating rock wall. Resist the temptation to outflank this obstacle as the surest route is to follow the polish up rock steps on big holds. The difficulties are short-lived and once behind you trending leftwards over shattered blocky rock will lead to the east ridge which is climbed airily to a large platform on Crib Goch's apparent summit (the true summit is half way along the ridge).

Spread out before you is a scene which is as beautiful as it is awe inspiring and one you will definitely want to photograph. Now is a good time to get your breath back, take in your surroundings and think about your shots as this is the only place on the ridge where it is practical to set up your gear. The view is one of 360 degrees so if you've arrived 'off peak' take your time and weigh up all your options before continuing your journey.

The ridge unfolds in spectacular fashion for 250 metres and is very exposed but with care can be traversed on the left hand (south) side using the crest as a handrail. As the ridge broadens the pinnacles arrive which can be passed on the left although it's better to climb them on good solid holds. If you've a friend with you then inspiring shots which impart the scale of the landscape can be had by sending them ahead to pose in improbable looking (but relatively safe) places.

Viewpoint 3 – Garnedd Ugain

After all the excitement of Crib Goch and the pinnacles descend to Bwlch Coch and give yourself a pat on the back; you made it! The next peak is Garnedd Ugain and to get there Crib y Ddysgl must be tackled and while much tamer than Crib Goch it is an excellent ridge in its own right. The way forward is a mixture of easy walking on clear paths interspersed with rock steps which should be taken as directly as you're comfortable with. The idea is to stay as close to the crest of the ridge as possible so try not to be seduced by false paths on the left flank which lead to dead ends. After a kilometre of tremendous ridge walking Garnedd Ugain's trig point appears on the skyline. This is the time to get your camera out and start prowling around the summit. Once again there is interest in 360 degrees but there is gold to be found in a retrospective view of Crib y Ddysgl and Crib Goch along with an intimate portrait of Snowdon's summit cone buttressed by the Clogwyn y Garnedd/Trinity Face.

Top: VP 2. A beautiful November dawn on Crib Goch. 4 shot stitched panorama.
Canon 6D, 24-70 at 24mm, ISO 100, 0.8 sec at f/11, 0.9 graduated filter, tripod.

Bottom: VP 1. The peaks of the horseshoe in the blue hour of pre-dawn – February.
Canon 6D, 24-70mm at 24mm, ISO 100, 15 sec at f/11, 0.6 – 0.9 graduated filters, tripod.

VP 3. Evening light on Crib a Ddysgl – June. 4 shot stitched panorama. Canon 7D, 17-40mm at 17mm, ISO 100, 1/20 sec at f/8, 0.9 graduated filter, tripod.

VP 3. Low cloud gathering around Yr Wyddfa – June evening. Canon 7D, 17-40mm at 17mm, ISO 100, 1/10 sec at f/11, 0.6 – 0.9 graduated filters, tripod.

Opposite: VP 4. Y Lliwedd above a temperature inversion from Yr Wyddfa – February evening. Canon 7D, 17-40mm at 17mm, ISO 100, 1/6 sec at f/11, 0.6 – 0.9 graduated filters, tripod.

Next Spread: *VP 5. Cat Evans enjoying the exposure of Bwlch Main on a July evening. Six shot stitched panorama. Canon 7D, 17-40mm at 17mm, ISO 100, 1/6 sec at f/8, 0.9 graduated filter.*

Viewpoint 4 – Yr Wyddfa summit

It's time for the highpoint of the day, Yr Wyddfa, the summit of Snowdon. Leave Garnedd Ugain and follow the cairned path which, at a prominent finger-stone, meets up with the Pig Track and the Llanberis Path along with the mountain railway. A short walk leads to the highest ground in England and Wales with everything that entails. The summit itself is not an easy place to shoot from but dropping down slightly (take great care on the eastern side) can make life a little easier. In the midst of all the hubbub and jostling it's up to you to make it work here on this, the loftiest of all vantage points.

Viewpoint 5 – To the pass of the arrows

Leave the summit in a south westerly direction until coming upon another finger-stone. Turn left and descend the steep and eroded upper reaches of the Watkin path. Take it steady and before too long you'll be safely down to Bwlch y Saethau, the fabled site of King Arthur's final battle. A much better path continues to the start of the climb up Y Lliwedd but it's worth bearing left and following the rim the cwm where you'll find small pools and a rocky ridge with excellent foregrounds for both Y Lliwedd and Yr Wyddfa which now stand high above you.

VP 2. Bwlch Main, Yr Aran and Moel Hebog from below the summit of Yr Wyddfa – March evening.
Canon 7D, 17-40mm at 17mm, ISO 100, 1/5 sec at f/8, 0.9 graduated filter, tripod.

07 THE SNOWDON HORSESHOE

Viewpoint 6 – The conquest of Y Lliwedd

Back on the Watkin path a large cairn indicates its continuation and descent into Cwm Llan. Our way goes straight ahead and follows a winding course all the way up onto Y Lliwedd's west peak but it is also possible (and recommended) to scramble up by keeping to the left and enjoying airy positions overlooking Llyn Llydaw and Y Lliwedd's awesome north face. Y Lliwedd's west peak is marginally higher than its eastern twin but both are wonderful belvederes affording a grandstand view of the whole route. Photographically there are possibilities for panoramas, long lens studies and the perfect opportunity for catching figures perched high on either of the summits.

Viewpoint 7 – Llyn Llydaw

After leaving Y Lliwedd's east peak follow the ridge on a clear path and down the occasional rocky step. After passing Lliwedd Bach the ground levels out where a cairn signals the way down into Cwm Dyli which is easy to follow but quite steep and scrambly in places. Before long the angle eases and the path continues over a wooden footbridge to the shores of Llyn Llydaw. This large glacial lake is a landscape photographer's paradise surrounded by towering peaks, replete with lagoon-like inlets and if you are lucky a mirror-still or even frozen surface. It's a fitting place to sit and contemplate your day and cap it off with some bonus images before joining the Miner's path and following it without incident all the way back to Pen y Pass.

It's been a day to remember … happy processing!

Opposite: VP 5. Cloud engulfing Y Lliwedd's North Face – October afternoon. Canon 6D, 24-70mm at 24mm, ISO 100, 1/10 sec at f/11, 0.9 graduated filter, tripod.

Left: VP 6. Lucie Sedlarova on Y Lliwedd's western peak with Yr Wyddfa and Garnedd Ugain beyond – March morning. Canon 7D, 17-40mm at 17mm, ISO 100, 1/160 sec at f/11, 0.6 graduated filters.

VP 7. Yr Wyddfa and Crib Goch from Llyn Llydaw – October afternoon. 6 shot stitched panorama. Canon 6D, 24-70mm at 24mm, ISO 100, 1/8 sec at f/11, 0.9 graduated filter, circular polariser, tripod.

VP 7. Winter moonlight at Llyn Llydaw – January. Six shot stitched panorama. Canon 6D, 24-70mm at 24mm, ISO 200, 30 sec at f/4, tripod.

08 MOEL EILIO AND LLYN DU'R ARDDU

Moel Eilio is a much-loved training ground for local fell runners, a 'mopping up' operation for list tickers and a constant backdrop to the lives of 'Llanberisians' on whom it smiles down from cradle to grave. To almost everyone else it is a nondescript hump languishing in obscurity as the western outpost of the Snowdon massif. A glamorous mountain it is not, but when taken as the first port of call on a wonderful rollercoaster ridge walk its ascent becomes a satisfying preliminary to three unbroken miles of airy perambulation.

Photographically this walk really delivers the goods with a wide variety of subjects and compositional possibilities. From Llanberis' bustling and colourful streets the route makes its way onto a broad ridge where distant views of mountain, valley and lake set the scene before a profoundly affecting finale beside Llyn Du'r Arddu in surroundings that are as impressive as any the British Isles can offer.

VP 5. A stream works its way down to Llyn Du'r Arddu on a beautiful July evening.
Canon 6D, 24-70mm at 24mm, ISO 100, 1/6 sec
at f/11, tripod, 0.9 graduated filter.

08 MOEL EILIO AND LLYN DU'R ARDDU

The walk

From the car park beside Llyn Padarn cross the road and walk up Market Street which leads onto High Street, the bustling hub of the village where colourful buildings form a slightly surreal setting for the comings and goings of locals and visitors alike. Turning left at the famous 'Pete's Eats' follow High Street for 300 metres before taking a right turn onto Capel Coch Road. Beyond the imposing chapel turn right onto Fron Goch and then the second left signed Plas Garnedd. The single-track road climbs steadily passing a number of ruined cottages on the way which make for interesting photographs. At the top of the road turn left onto a bridleway and stay with it for 300 metres before heading uphill towards a stile in the left-hand corner of the field. It's time to hit the hills!

Viewpoint 1 – The slops of Moel Eilio

Beyond the stile a grassy ridge will take you to the top of Moel Eilio with a little bit of effort but no difficulties whatsoever. On this ascent there is a tendency is to stick to the right-hand side of the wall/fence but to do so would be to miss out on some excellent photographic opportunities. Another stile is soon encountered which enables you to swap sides and roam at will. Behind you the view of Llanberis and Elidir Fawr gets better with every step and higher up an investigation of the edges of the ridge will bring Llyn Dwythwch within the range of your camera.

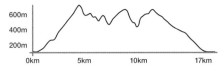

ELEVATION: Lowest: 106m   Highest: 726m   Total ascent: 1197.6m

DISTANCE: 10.5 miles / 17 kilometres

VP 1. Nature reclaiming an old farmstead on the way to Moel Eilio on a February afternoon. Canon 7D, 17-40mm at 22mm, ISO 100, 100 sec at f/8.

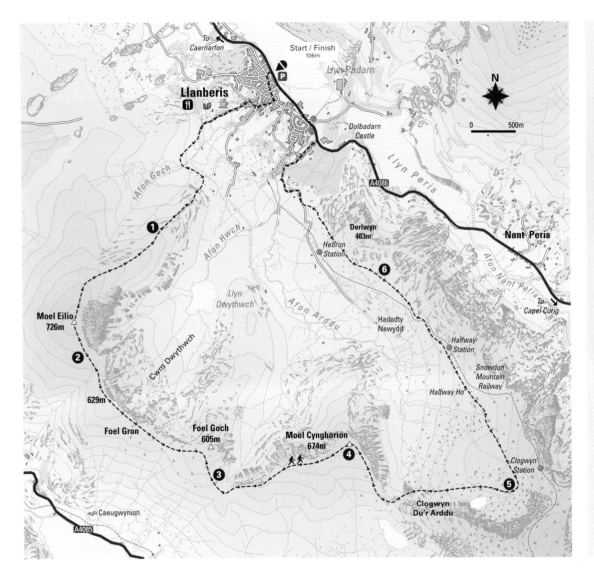

How to get here

The walk starts in Llanberis, from the large car park on the A4086 beside Llyn Padarn 8 miles from Caernarfon and 11 miles from Capel Curig.

Parking postcode: LL55 4ER
Parking grid ref: SH 57775 60482
Parking lat/long: 53.120792, -4.125991
Map: OS Explorer Map OL17 (1:25 000) Snowdon/Conwy Valley

Accessibility

This is a strenuous mountain walk of 10.5 miles / 17km with 1200 metres of ascent. The paths are generally faint on the ground but fences along the entire length of the Moel Eilio ridge act as fool proof navigational aids should poor visibility occur. The short ascent to Llyn Du'r Arddu requires a sure foot and the return leg to Llanberis is on a well-made 'tourist path' which is easy to follow in all but the very worst winter conditions. The walk can be cut short just beyond Foel Goch at Bwlch Maesgwm where a bridleway can be picked up and followed back to the start.

Best time of year/day

Photographically this walk comes into its own at the end of the day with unobstructed golden hour light year-round. From dawn to dusk throughout the year changeable weather, sunshine and showers, can be considered excellent conditions for capturing dramatic images. Clogwyn Du'r Arddu catches late light a couple of weeks either side of the summer solstice and then remains in shadow for the rest of the year. In full winter conditions the usual caveats apply regarding ice axe, crampons and experience in their use.

Opposite top: VP 1. Llyn Dwythwch, the Glyderau and Snowdon from the flanks of Moel Eilio on an evening in May. Four shot stitched panorama. Canon 7D, 17-40mm at 17mm, ISO 100, 1.3 sec at f/11, tripod, 0.6 graduated filter.

VP 2. Looking towards Snowdon from Moel Eilio late on a February afternoon. Four shot stitched panorama. Canon 6D, 24-70mm at 24mm, ISO 100, 1/25 sec at f/8, 0.9 graduated filter, tripod.

VP 2. Snowdon and the Moel Eilio ridge illuminated by late December light. Canon 6D, 24-70mm at 24mm, ISO 100, 1/20 sec at f/11, 0.9 graduated filter.

Viewpoint 2 – Moel Eilio

Moel Eilio's palatial summit shelter is the perfect place to get your breath back, take in an expanded vista and gird your loins for what lies ahead. A fence runs the length of the summit ridge and is an indispensable compositional tool of which you should make full use. You'll notice that the peaks of the Eifionydd have sprung into view but hold your fire as better vantage points await. The sprawling nature of the summit suggests sweeping panoramas but it's worth employing longer focal lengths to pull in distant ranges such as the Glyderau which peeps over the minor peaks of the Llanberis ridge.

Viewpoint 3 – Foel Goch

The walk really gets going now and from Moel Eilio all the way to Foel Goch things become aesthetically more pleasing. On Foel Gron the outlook is enhanced by the sudden appearance of Llyn Cwellyn which adds much interest to a huge vista backed by the Hebog, Nantlle and Mynydd Mawr ranges. Outcropping rocks provide foreground interest and subtle positioning of your camera is key to achieving balanced compositions. The descent from Foel Goch to Bwlch Maesgwm is steep but thankfully short and once there you have a choice to make.

Viewpoint 4 – Moel Cynghorion

At Bwlch Maesgwm and after many ups and downs it might be tempting to drop onto the Snowdon Ranger path until the next pass is reached. Do resist the temptation as the ascent of Moel Cynghorion is steady going and has lots to offer the photographer. Near the top of the first steep section a collection of large erratic boulders will have you setting up and forgetting the toil of the climb. These act as great foregrounds to the Hebog range across the valley. The ridge now lies back at a more forgiving angle and the walk becomes a breezy promenade across a vast sheep run. Just beyond the meagre summit cairn the ground falls away dramatically and from across the abyss comes an unusual perspective on Clogwyn Du'r Arddu and Cwm Clogwyn with 'Hafod Eryri', usually replete with tiny figures, rising high above. Beyond the stile comes another steep descent to where the 'Ranger' path hoiks itself via a series of zig zags towards the crowded roof of Wales.

VP 3. The Moel Hebog group from Bwlch Maesgwm on a showery December afternoon.
Canon 6D, 24-70mm at 17mm, ISO 100, 1/320 sec at f/7.1, 0.6 and 0.9 graduated filters.

Viewpoint 5 – Clogwyn Du'r Arddu

Things now take a very different turn. From the lowest point of the bwlch go left over a stile and follow a faint trod below a damp, vegetated crag before reaching the remains of an old wall. Here the path gives up the ghost but a rising leftward traverse over very rough and bouldery terrain soon brings you to the outflow of Llyn Du'r Arddu. You are now in one of the most sublime mountain landscapes imaginable and your mission is to explore it. Everything you need for compelling images is here. Clogwyn Du'r Arddu rears up as an unnerving, architectonic wall of rock, the llyn shelves steeply away into unknown copper-blue fathoms and water courses will entice you in your efforts to find the perfect compositions. The environs of Llyn Du'r Arddu are the photographic climax of this walk but to unlock the best that this remarkable haven has to offer will take time and repeated visits.

Opposite top: VP 4. Slow Train Coming – The Snowdon Railway and Glyder Fawr from Moel Cynghorion on an evening in June. Canon 6D, 24-70mm at 70mm, ISO 100, 1/50 sec at f/7.1, 0.9 graduated filter.

Middle: VP 4. Cloggy looming out of the mist on a January afternoon. Canon 7D, 17-40mm at 17mm, ISO 100, 1/25 sec at f/8, tripod, 0.9 graduated filter.

Bottom: VP 4. A June evening on Moel Cynghorion. Canon 6D, 24-70mm at 24mm, ISO 100, 1/10 sec at f/10, tripod, 0.9 graduated filter.

VP 5. Clogwyn Du'r Arddu on an evening in June. Canon 6D, 24-70mm at 26mm, ISO 100, 1/20 sec at f/11, tripod, 0.9 graduated filter.

08 MOEL EILIO AND LLYN DU'R ARDDU

Viewpoint 6 – Back to town

When you finally manage to drag yourself away the easiest way of reaching the Llanberis path is to start from the rock-strewn moraine above the lake and head north until the unmistakeable 'Llanberis motorway' is underfoot. Although your immediate surroundings are tame in comparison to what has gone before there is still scope for image gathering especially above the path where the Snowdon Railway can be seen snaking away into the distance giving a strong leading line back to 'Cloggy'. The way back to your starting point follows the path which after passing the Pen y Ceunant Café descends a steep tarmac road to Victoria Terrace. If your legs are tired on this last descent then try walking backwards, it really helps. From the mini roundabout at the end of the terrace turn left and follow the road for 1km back to the car park or, you could stop for a pint in 'The Heights' … you've earned it.

VP 6. Evening mist forming around 'Cloggy' on a July evening.
Canon 7D, 17-40mm at 17mm, ISO 100, 1/25 sec at f/8,
tripod, 0.6 graduated filter.

09 THE NANTLLE RIDGE

If you believe that all of Snowdonia's finest upland vistas have been done to death then here is a walk on which to recalibrate your perceptions. Sitting between Snowdon and the sea in the old cantref of Eifionydd the exquisitely sculpted Nantlle Ridge is an anomaly in that it sees relatively few visitors but ranks as one of the most rewarding mountain photography walks in the national park. Those who seek out inspiring landscapes are well catered for on Nantlle's soaring crest but beyond the manifold aesthetic attractions the subtle magic of an area rich in folklore and fable accompanies every traverse of these elegant peaks.

This walk introduces the concept of 'future classics'. Strong mountain images can be made along the entire length of a ridge which has yet to be fully exploited by the photographic community. This gives you the opportunity to explore somewhere a little different and put your own stamp on a series of largely undiscovered locations.

VP 1. Moel Hebog, Mynydd Drws y Coed and the Nantlle Ridge on a glorious May evening. Two shot stitched panorama. Canon 6D, 24-70mm at 24mm, ISO 100, 1/4 sec at f/11, tripod, 0.9 graduated filter.

09 THE NANTLLE RIDGE

The walk

From the car park at Rhyd Ddu cross the road and go through an iron gate onto a well-made path which forms part of the 'Lon Las Gwyrfai', a pleasant low-level ramble which threads its way through the forest all the way to Beddgelert. Shortly after crossing the footbridge take the right fork and when the path meets the B4418 go left through a gate and carry on over a couple of stiles onto the open mountain.

From here a steep and unremitting slog will eventually land you on the broad summit of Y Garn. A faint trod trends right across a boulder field to another stile over which two large cairn-shelters provide a choice as to which one you would like to collapse into.

Viewpoint 1 – Y Garn

Y Garn is a splendid viewpoint but like other large plateau-like areas it can be difficult to convey a sense of height in a photograph. Fortunately, the ground falls steeply away on three sides, most precipitously to the east and north where dizzying bird's eye views of the valleys below along with the Snowdon range and Mynydd Mawr respectively await those with a good head for heights. On the western margins of the plateau the rest of your route is laid out before you with Mynydd Drws y Coed taking centre stage and rising sheer into the sky like an enormous shark's fin, a scene that is as beautiful as it is impressive and one that really comes to life on spring and summer evenings. Away from the edges the wall that runs along the length of Y Garn can be used as an effective leading line for compositions which include Mynydd Drws y Coed.

How to get here

Start point – The main Rhyd Ddu car park is at the southern end of the Rhyd Ddu village on the A4085, 3.2 miles from Beddgelert, and 5.5 miles from Waunfawr.

End point – From the Rhyd Ddu car park turn right on the A4085 and turn left beyond the Cwellyn Arms. Follow the road all the way to Nantlle village. Once past Llyn Nantlle Uchaf the road bends to the right and after one kilometre at a Talysarn turn left. After 1.5 kilometres turn left again and follow the single track road all the way to its end. Go through the gate and park up.

Parking postcode:	Start point LL54 6TN
	End point LL54 6RT
Parking grid ref:	Start point SH 57103 52563
	End point SH 49535 51063
Parking lat/long:	Start point 53.054593, -4.136262
	End point 53.035635, -4.245494
Map:	OS Explorer Map OL17 (1:25 000)
	Snowdon/Conwy Valley

Accessibility

This is a moderately challenging walk of just under 7 miles / 11km with 980 metres of ascent. The linear nature of this expedition means that two cars placed strategically at either end are required to complete the whole route. If that is not possible then the walk can be shortened at either Trum y Ddysgl or Mynydd Tal y Mignedd by descending their southern ridges and returning back to Rhyd Ddu via Bwlch Ddwy Elor and the Beddgelert Forest. The paths are grassy and easy going throughout apart from the short avoidable scramble up Mynydd Drws y Coed which can be greasy if at all damp. Proximity to the sea and relatively low altitude mean that barring exceptional winters it is rarely adversely affected by snow and ice conditions for which, when they do occur, the usual caveats apply.

Best time of year/day

The east/west configuration of the ridge makes it a good year-round target for golden hour photography. For strong walkers a double traverse is an option which is especially rewarding during the autumn and winter months when advantage can be taken of both early and late light.

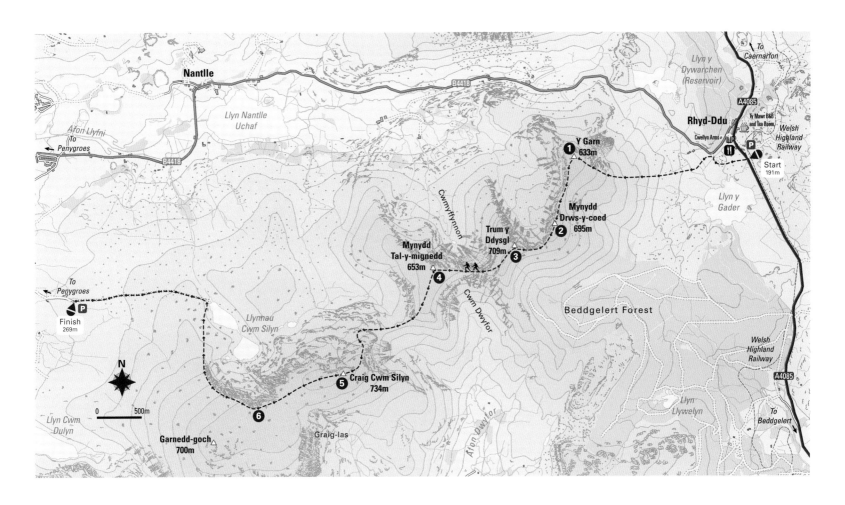

Nantlle

Llyn Nantlle
Uchaf

Afon Llyfni
To
Penygroes

B4418

B4418

To
Penygroes

Finish
269m

Llynnau
Cwm Silyn

N

0   500m

Llyn Cwm
Dulyn

Craig Cwm Silyn
734m

5

6

Garnedd-goch
700m

Graig-las

Llyn y
Dywarchen
(Reservoir)

To
Caernarfon

A4085

Rhyd-Ddu

Ty Mawr B&B
and Tea Room

Cwellyn Arms

i

P

Start
191m

Welsh
Highland
Railway

Llyn y
Gader

Y Garn
633m

1

Mynydd
Drws-y-coed
695m

2

Cwmffynnon

Trum y
Ddysgl
709m

3

Mynydd
Tal-y-mignedd
653m

4

Cwm Dwyfor

Beddgelert Forest

Welsh
Highland
Railway

A4085

Llyn
Llywelyn

To
Beddgelert

Afon Dwyfor

ELEVATION: Lowest: 191m   Highest: 734m   Total ascent: 982.9m

DISTANCE: 6.8 miles / 11 kilometres

600m
400m
200m

0km   5km   11km

VP 1. Snowdon appearing out of the clouds from Y Garn on an April afternoon. Canon 6D, 24-70mm at 70mm, ISO 100, 1/200 sec at f/8, 0.9 graduated filter.

Opposite: *VP 1. Mynydd Drws y Coed on a wild and stormy May afternoon.
Canon 6D, 24-70mm at 70mm, ISO 100, 1/200 sec at f/11.*

Viewpoint 2 – Mynydd Drws y Coed

The scramble onto Mynydd Drws y Coed is not as daunting as it first appears. From Y Garn keep to the right-hand side of the wall and make your way up and over short rock steps which can be taken direct or avoided on the left. The summit is a slender grassy walkway with a profound abyss on its north-western aspect. The lie of the land here makes it an ideal place for dramatic 'figures in the landscape' compositions. Simply put, this is a wonderful place to be and it shouldn't be too difficult to persuade your companions to hang around so you can capture them for posterity.

Viewpoint 3 – Trum y Ddysgl

The route to your next peak crosses an old fence before dropping down to a deep col. A good path ascends easily to the top but for maximum thrills stay on the apex of the delectable grass arete. The summit of Trum y Ddysgl is another flat plateau and is not in itself the most exciting of places. However, it's all about the views which are tremendous. Looking south the Moelwynion and Hebog ranges make for great panoramic images while to the north and across the cwm Snowdon can be seen peeping over the top of Mynydd Drws y Coed. To the south west Mynydd Tal y Mignedd and Craig Cwm Silyn fill the midground with the Irish Sea beyond. In terms of foregrounds Trum y Ddysgl disappoints but as with Y Garn they are not necessary as expansive compositions are the order of the day.

Viewpoint 4 – Mynydd Tal y Mignedd

Beyond Trum y Ddysgl a short descent leads to a lovely little ridge where softer rock has eroded to form a distinct notch which requires care in the wet. A thankfully short re-ascent then places you on the summit of Mynydd Tal y Mignedd. This is, photographically, the least interesting peak but does provide the best vantage point for Craig y Bera, the shattered, gully-riven crags that cling precariously to Mynydd Mawr's south face. A curious feature of the summit is the drystone obelisk which can be seen from afar throughout the ridge traverse and was built to commemorate Queen Victoria's diamond jubilee. This is a great place for a bite to eat in preparation for the final push of the day.

Viewpoint 5 – Craig Cwm Silyn

The way down to Bwlch Dros-bern is awkward, steep and slippery when wet but with a steady approach it is soon behind you. Ahead lies a buttress of rough, broken rock up which experienced scramblers will find great pleasure in forging a route. An easier way with no technical difficulties finds its way on a narrow heathery path which swings to the right of steeper ground gaining height steadily before trending leftwards to re-join the ridge. The summit of Craig Cwm Silyn is soon underfoot and discloses the twists and turns of your journey to perfection. Wide shots and panoramas are the obvious choice here as the view is quite sublime but tighter compositions should also be contemplated in order to capitalise on the shapes and forms which make up the various peaks and connecting ridges.

Top left: VP 2. Lucie Sedlarova admiring the view from Mynydd Drws y Coed on a May afternoon. Canon 7D, 17-40mm at 17mm, ISO 100, 1/200 sec at f/11.

Top right: VP 2. Moel Hebog from Mynydd Drws y Coed on a March afternoon. Canon 6D, 24-70mm at 42mm, ISO 100, 1/100 sec at f/11, 0.9 graduated filter.

Bottom left: VP 2. Looking south towards Moel Hebog and the Moelwynion from Mynydd Drws y Coed on a November evening. Canon 6D, 24-70mm at 24mm, ISO 100, 0.5 sec at f/11, tripod, 0.9 graduated filter.

Bottom left: VP 2. Dave Dear capturing the scene from Mynydd Drws y Coed on a March afternoon. Canon 6D, 24-70mm at 24mm, ISO 100, 1/60 sec at f/11, 0.6 and 0.9 graduated filters.

VP 4. April afternoon storm light on Mynydd Mawr from Mynydd Tal y Mignedd. Canon 6D, 24-70mm at 44mm, ISO 100, 1/50 sec at f/11.

VP 5. Mynydd Tal y Mignedd and Trum y Ddysgl from Craig Cwm Silyn on an evening in April. Canon 6D, 24-70mm at 70mm, ISO 100, 1/250 sec at f/8, 0.9 graduated filter.

Viewpoint 6 – The way down

From Craig Cwm Silyn's stony top head WSW keeping the plunging declivities of Craig yr Ogof well to your right until a stile grants access to the long curving arm that eventually leads to the improbably blue Llynnau Cwm Silyn. You are now confronted with a vision of craggy magnificence reminiscent of the Glyderau in all its savage glory. From high above the cwm floor the 'Great Slab' is seen head on and if you are lucky there will be climbers in situ to impart its true scale. Get your longest lens on and zoom in on the action. Panoramic images also work well here as there is a lot to take in and even the widest lens falls short in including the cwm with its crags and lakes in context.

Viewpoint 7 – Llynnau Cwm Silyn

The day is almost over but there is one more 'must-visit' location before you call time on what has been a superb photographic expedition. If visibility is good you will have spotted the twin lakes of Llynnau Cwm Silyn from above. It is now just a simple matter of following the ridge down to them over easy ground. The outflow of the nethermost lake is the spot to aim for and there you will find plenty of rocks to aid your compositions. There can be few finer places to set up a tripod and relax after an epic day in the mountains and never more so than during the summer months when late light floods into the cwm. With the show over, walk through the gate and enjoy a gentle stroll down the old cart track back to your car.

Opposite: *VP 3. Two walkers making their way to Trum y Ddysgl from Mynydd Tal y Mignedd on an April afternoon. Canon 6D, 24-70mm at 37mm, ISO 100, 1/80 sec at f/8, 0.6 and 0.9 graduated filters.*

Left: *VP 3. Snowdon peeping over Mynydd Drws y Coed from Trum y Ddysgl on a November evening. Canon 6D, 24-70mm at 70mm, ISO 100, 0.5 sec at f/11, tripod, 0.6 graduated filter.*

VP 6. Llynnau Cwm Silyn and the great slab of Craig yr Ogof on an April evening. Four shot stitched panorama. Canon 6D, 24-70mm at 24mm, ISO 100, 1/25 sec at f/8, 0.6 graduated filter.

VP 7. A still April dusk beside Llynnau Cwm Silyn. Four shot stitched panorama. Canon 7D, 17-40mm at 17mm, ISO 100, 3.2 sec at f/11, tripod, 0.6 graduated filter.

10 MOEL Y DYNIEWYD AND THE AFON GLASLYN

As landscape photographers we often have a theme in mind when considering a day out with our camera. On some days we'll want to shoot lakeside scenes and on others we may decide a quiet hilltop with far reaching views is the order of the day. Occasionally we'll find ourselves drawn to a fast flowing mountain stream or perhaps the call of the wild will lead us off the beaten track in search of adventure and new horizons. With variety being the spice of life wouldn't it be nice if there was a route that incorporated all these elements? The good news is that those who seek a diverse range of subject matter need look no further than this excellent itinerary which ticks all the boxes and more besides.

Starting in the fairytale village of Beddgelert this meandering circuit takes in the impressive Aberglaslyn Gorge and then discovers a hidden valley where rusting remnants stand as a reminder of the copper industry of yesteryear. A seldom trodden mini mountain surrounded by well-loved peaks provides stunning panoramic views before a rollercoaster ridge takes us into a secluded haven where Scots pines gather on a rocky knoll. Then, via a gorgeous birchwood, we descend to Llyn Dinas and then back to the start along the Afon Glaslyn which begins its life high on Snowdon. Ice cream to finish the day? It would be rude not to.

VP 4. Bryn Castell on a September afternoon.
Canon 6D, 24-70 at 35mm, ISO 100, 1/15 sec at f/11, tripod, 0.9 graduated filter.

10 MOEL Y DYNIEWYD AND THE AFON GLASLYN

The walk

Leave the car park and turn left down the road (resisting the temptation to visit the ice cream parlour) before joining the lane to the left of Ty Isaf. Just beyond the public toilets turn right through a gate which joins a pleasant if uneventful riverside path.

Stick with the path which via a foot bridge crosses the Welsh Highland Railway line. From here to Pont Aberglaslyn the path hugs the bank of the Afon Glaslyn with an admirable tenacity and the scene grows more spectacular with every step. This is a very special place reminiscent of an Himalayan gorge in miniature.

Viewpoint 1 – Pass of Afon Glaslyn
There are many opportunities along the way to shoot from the water's edge but care must be taken as the rocks can be very greasy and the river becomes a potentially dangerous torrent when in spate. To those with an interest in steam trains the locomotives of the WHR regularly pass through the gorge before disappearing into a tunnel enabling you to capture charming images which evoke a bygone age. As the path meets the road at Pont Aberglaslyn a stepped path on the left heads into the woods and before long arrives at the National Trust Nantmor car park. Before taking the path, however, head onto the bridge itself for a wonderful view down the gorge which is especially beautiful in Autumn. With care and due consideration to other road users this location can yield fantastic images.

VP 4. The Afon Glaslyn tumbling through an autumnal Aberglaslyn Gorge, November mornin
Canon 6D, 24-70mm at 29mm, ISO 100, 0.8 sec at f/16, tripod, polarising filter, 0.6 graduated filter.

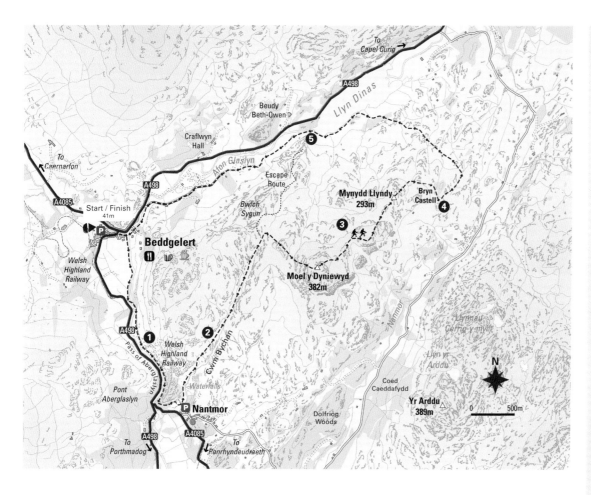

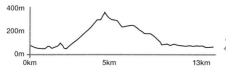

ELEVATION: Lowest: 41m   Highest: 382m   Total ascent: 445m

DISTANCE: 8.3 miles / 13 kilometres

How to get here

Parking can be found in the SNPA car park next to the Royal Goat Hotel in Beddgelert. Beddgelert can be reached on the A4085 13 miles from Caernarfon, the A4086/A498 11 miles from Capel Curig and the A498 8 miles from Porthmadog.

Parking postcode: LL55 4YE
Parking grid ref: SH588 481
Parking lat/long: 53.011447, -4.106269
Map: OS Explorer Map OL17 (1:25 000) Snowdon / Conwy Valley

Accessibility

This is a moderate hill walk of 8.3 miles / 13km with 610 metres of ascent. Much of the route is on excellent paths but from Moel y Dyniewyd to Bryn Castell paths are faint and traverse rough heather-clad hillsides. For those wishing to shorten the route a direct descent to Llyn Dinas can be made from Bwlch Sygun. Winter conditions are rare but in the event of snow and ice the route can usually be enjoyed without axe or crampons but becomes more strenuous and requires care on ascents and descents. Bracken chokes the immediate environs of Bryn Castell in the summer months so be on guard for and know how to deal with sheep ticks.

Best time of year/day

Moel y Dyniewyd and its surrounding hill slopes come into their own during late summer when the heather is at its best. Late light is good all year round. With so much woodland to enjoy on this route autumn is the prime time to visit. Llyn Dinas is an accessible location for sunrise shoots and its waters are ripple free more often than almost any other lake in the area.

VP 1. A may evening beside the Afon Glaslyn. Canon 7D, 17-40mm at 17mm, ISO 100, 0.5 sec at f/14, tripod.

VP 3. Snowdon from Moel y Dyniewyd on an August evening. Canon 6D, 24-70mm at 24mm, ISO 100, 1/5 sec at f/16, tripod, 0.6 graduated filter.

VP 3. Cnicht and the Moelwynion from Moel y Dyniewyd – September evening. Canon 6D, 24-70mm at 26mm, ISO 100, 0.5 sec at f/16, 0.6 graduated filter, tripod.

10 MOEL Y DYNIEWYD AND THE AFON GLASLYN

Viewpoint 2 – Cwm Bychan

From the Nantmor car park pass beside the toilet block and under the railway bridge. The path climbs steadily through ancient woodland lush with mosses and lichens, a great place to indulge in macro photography. As you leave the woodland the path continues to climb and a nearby stream and its cascades can be investigated for another long exposure fix. Soon the valley (Cwm Bychan) becomes bare and austere with its steep sides bearing down on a number of old pylons, the forsaken infrastructure of the early 20th century copper mine which prove irresistible subjects for inspection and photography. Curiosity satisfied, carry on up the valley ignoring a small subsidiary cwm on the left before gaining Bwlch Sygun and a meeting of ways.

Viewpoint 3 – Moel y Dyniewyd and Mynydd Llyndy

For those with a distaste for rough mountain walking the route can be cut short here by picking up the path down to Llyn Dinas, an option worth considering if you wish to obtain an aerial view of the llyn. Red blooded walkers will turn right for an ascent of Moel y Dyniewyd and be richly rewarded for their efforts. The way to Dyniewyd's seldom trodden summit follows a fence and involves some steep sections where many have used it to aid progress. If this is your approach then proceed with caution as it is topped with rusty barbed wire. From the top the view

opens up considerably. This modest lump is surrounded by high mountains and big vista shots call out from all points of the compass. This is a sunset location to die for.

The next section keeps the fence to your left and heads out towards Mynydd Llyndy over an undulating heathery ridge on barely discernible paths giving the feeling that you're pioneering your way through the hills. The going is rough but extremely satisfying. Partway along the ridge a stile is ignored and keeping with the fence the way leads to a very steep descent which is circumvented by a detour to the right and a grassy gully with drops into a shallow bowl. Ahead lies the peak of Mynydd Llyndy which is ascended by skirting around the bowl and picking a way up a short pathless slope to rejoin the fence. After a short descent cross a stile and turn right to follow a wall passing through a gap and over another stile as you go. A little further on cross a broken section of wall on your right and brave tussocky ground to find somewhere to place your tripod.

VP 2. Cwm Bychan long exposure.
Canon 6D, 24-70mm at 24mm, ISO 100, 30 sec and f/11, tripod, 6 stop ND filter, 0.9 graduated filter.

VP 3. The Afon Glaslyn threading its way towards Beddgelert from Grib Ddu on the shortcut descent – November afternoon. Canon 7D, 17-40mm at 21mm, ISO 100, 1/50 sec at f/8, tripod, 0.9 graduated filter.

10 MOEL Y DYNIEWYD AND THE AFON GLASLYN

Viewpoint 4 – Bryn Castell

Bryn Castell is a rocky knoll topped with pines and is a prominent feature from many a distant view. As an obvious target for photographers it is rarely visited and one can only assume that difficulty of access is the reason. Congratulations, you're one of the few to put this sublime feature in front of your camera. There are many interesting trees to shoot in this part of the Llyndy Isaf estate and it would not be difficult to spend many hours here exploring all the options available.

To continue, cross the stile beneath the 'Bryn' and walk a short distance NE to pick up a grassy track then turn left at a 'crossroads' and go through the gate that leads to Hafod Owen, an idyllic whitewashed cottage which was once the home of John Menlove Edwards, a brilliant but tragic figure who put up many classic rock climbs in the 1930s. This little homestead backed by the Snowdon massif really is a sight to see on an autumn afternoon. A stile is crossed to the right of Hafod Owen and gives access to an fairy tale path which weaves up and around hillocks peppered with birch. Could this be Snowdonia's answer to Holme Fell in the Lake District?

Viewpoint 5 – Llyn Dinas

One last treat is in store before the return march to Beddgelert and that well earned ice cream. Descending steeply through woodland you soon find yourself beside Llyn Dinas, one of the prettiest and most tranquil lakes in North Wales. Once there you'll need no instruction on what to shoot, just get stuck in as you make your way around to the south west tip and the path which takes you back to Beddgelert in a blissful 2.8km.

Top: VP 3. The Snowdon Massif from below the summit of Moel y Dyniewyd. December afternoon. Canon 6D, 24-70mm at 24mm, ISO 100, 1/15 sec at f/11, tripod, 0.9 graduated filter.

Left: VP 4. A gloomy September afternoon near Bryn Castell. Canon 6D, 24-70mm at 50mm, ISO 100, 1/8 sec at f/8, tripod, polarising filter, 0.6 graduated filter.

Overleaf: VP 5. A January dawn beside Llyn Dinas. Six shot stitched panorama. Canon 6D, 24-70mm at 24mm, ISO 100, 0.6 sec at f/11, tripod, polarising filter, 0.9 graduated filter.

11 THE NANTMOR SKYLINE

Withdrawn and hidden from prying eyes the timeless valley of Nantmor is a Snowdonian Shangri la ignored by the masses and frequented, when at all, by those with a predilection for wild and lonely places. There you'll find a scattering of cottages nestling beneath unkempt slopes of heather and hawthorn where, on an autumn afternoon, it is hard to imagine a more romantic idyll. To the north west a network of footpaths may tempt you to unsuspected places of great charm but from the craggy heights in the south the wind whispers "come hither", a request to which, as a mountain photographer, you will feel duty bound to respond.

A walk tracing Nantmor's south eastern skyline should be an obvious target but few feet venture further than the ever popular Cnicht, beyond which a complex hinterland of rocky protuberances and secretive pools invite exploration. Of all the routes in this book this is the one that most richly rewards an exploratory approach with a genuine sense of discovery in a landscape as fresh and unspoiled as it must have been 100 years ago.

Andrew Jones on Cnicht's eastern top during an atmospheric November afternoon.
Canon 6D, 24-70mm at 57mm, ISO 100, 1/15 sec at f/8, 0.9 graduated filter, tripod.

11 THE NANTMOR SKYLINE

The walk

From the parking area turn left and follow the road a short distance to Gelli Iago/the Nantmor Mountain Centre where a gate accesses the right of way which skirts left of and then behind the centre before crossing a footbridge over the tumbling waters of the Afon Gelli Iago.

Viewpoint 1 – Above Gelli Iago

A well-worn path now zig zags upwards quickly gaining height and within a few minutes a backward glance reveals a birds-eye view of Nantmor backed by the Snowdon range and the distant Glyderau. Further on and through a gate with a novel method of closure the stream will tempt your photographic eye down to the water's edge where compositions can be worked all day long should the compulsion overcome you.

Viewpoint 2 – Llynnau Cerrig y Myllt and Llyn Arddu

Back to business. Through a gap in a tumbledown wall and just past some stepping stones it is time to leave the beaten track and turn right onto pathless ground where one of two stiles will soon be encountered. You are now entering the environs of Yr Arddu and bereft of distinct trails a south westerly course will take you to the Llynnau Cerrig y Myllt, two stunning lakelets cradled in heathery bowls. The scenery hereabouts is reminiscent of the Rhinogydd and it is up to you how much time you dedicate to exploring this maze-like area of rocky wilderness. From the southernmost lake head south west through a mini 'canyon' and then across damp ground until you come to Llyn Arddu, a lake so wild and beautiful that you'll wonder why it hasn't been photographed to death. An absolutely sublime spot.

*VP 1. The Afon Gelli Iago on an April evening.
Canon 6D, 24-70mm at 30mm, ISO 100, 0.3 sec at f/16, tripod,
polarising filter, 0.6 graduated filter.*

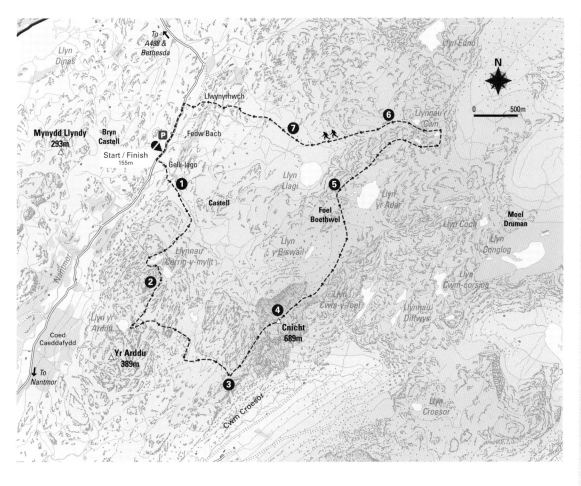

ELEVATION: Lowest: 155m Highest: 689m Total ascent: 874.5m

DISTANCE: 7.4 miles / 12 kilometres

How to get here

The Nantmor Mountain Centre or Gelli Iago is just over a mile down a single track road just off the A498 in between Llyn Gwynant and Llyn Dinas. If travelling from Beddgelert take the first right after Llyn Dinas or, if coming from Capel Curig take the first left after the Pont Bethania car park/Caffi Gwynant.

Parking postcode: LL55 4NL
Parking grid ref: SH 63255 48467
Parking lat/long: 53.016511, -4.039389
Map: OS Explorer Map OL17 (1:25 000) Snowdon / Conwy Valley

Accessibility

This is a strenuous mountain walk of 7.4 miles / 12km with 870 metres of ascent. Paths range from very good to vague or non-existent and in poor visibility your navigation skills will be put fully to the test. A range of terrain is encountered including road walking, heather bashing, scrambling and bog trotting. Gaiters are recommended. Winter rarely presents undue dangers or difficulties on this walk but in snow and ice conditions the ascent to Cnicht's summit should be treated with caution as should be the traverse of Craig Llyn Llagi.

Best time of year/day

This is a great year-round walk which comes into its own later in the day. Cnicht in particular is great sunset location. Mid to late summer sees the heather in bloom on Yr Arddu and during spring and autumn the woodland in the latter stages of the walk is especially pleasing.

VP 2. Cnicht and the Moelwynion from Yr Arddu on a March afternoon of sunshine and showers. Canon 7D, 17-40mm at 17mm, ISO 100, 1/40 sec at f/11, tripod, 0.9 graduated filter.

VP 2. Llynnau Cerrig y Myllt with Snowdon beyond on an October evening. Canon 6D, 24-70mm at 24mm, ISO 100, 1/5 sec at f/11, tripod, 0.9 graduated filter.

11 THE NANTMOR SKYLINE

Viewpoint 3 – Approaching Cnicht

From the llyn retrace your steps to the damp area and turn right down a grassy break in the crags where the eagle-eyed will spot the 'Cnicht Hotel', a little 'howff' which affords basic shelter for the night. A faint trod heads south east into a narrowing where the path then follows a stream before striking out east through some bracken to an old quarry in a subsidiary valley. A short slog up the hillside passing a deep hole on the way lands you on Cnicht's west ridge. Until now the mountain has exhibited an unflattering broadside but here it finally assumes its famously pyramidal profile which has earned it the fanciful title of the 'Matterhorn of Wales'. A little off-piste wandering will reveal brand new perspectives and compositions for you to work with so be sure to have a good rummage around.

Viewpoint 4 – Cnicht

The way ahead follows the west ridge without deviation with the deep trench of Cwm Croesor on your right growing more impressive with every step until a grassy shelf replete with ergonomic rocks to sit upon offers a chance to gather yourself before the final assault on Cnicht's craggy nose. To the right of the obvious rock step (which gives a short grade 3 scramble to those of suitable ability) a narrow gully provides a very pleasant and easy clamber on big holds and meets a well-trodden path which climbs, via a couple of slatey grooves, to the top of the mountain. Drink in the exceptional 360-degree view and then wonder what you are going to do with it. In truth the summit rocks are arranged in such a way that conventional compositions can be tricky; if this proves too hard to handle then think telephoto, panoramic or even portrait orientation.

VP 3. Looking down Cnicht's western ridge to Porthmadog and the Irish Sea on an April evening. Four shot stitched panorama. Canon 6D, 24-70mm at 24mm, ISO 100, 1/10 sec at f/11, tripod, 0.6 and 0.9 graduated filters.

11 THE NANTMOR SKYLINE

Viewpoint 5 – Llyn yr Adar

The walk along Cnicht's slender summit ridge is pure poetry but once past the east top you enter an austere tract of peaty moorland which couldn't be more different to the airy skywalk you've just enjoyed. Continue along the broad, low-profile ridge until Llyn yr Adar comes into view around the spot height of 631m. This is your cue to start descending in a northerly direction to cross a boggy depression before arriving on the rock festooned ridge of Craig Llyn Llagi. The plunging views down to Llyn Llagi are breathtaking as is the voyage of discovery you about to embark on. Taking a north easterly course will see you on your way to Y Cyrniau and it is advisable to look around corners, climb onto outcrops and leave no stone unturned (figuratively speaking, of course) in your search for images. The immense backdrop of the Snowdon massif to your left and Moelwyn Mawr across the dark waters of Llyn yr Adar to your right give ample opportunities to practise your compositions and framing by using the many and varied foregrounds available to you.

Viewpoint 6 – Llynnau'r Cwn

From Y Cyrniau's highest point it's just a short hop east through hummocks and knolls to Llynnau'r Cwn, the 'Dog Lakes'. These three small pools are a favourite haunt of MLT (mountain leader training) expeditions and their discreet sunken location makes them an excellent wild camping spot but very difficult to successfully photograph. Worry not, for there is more water not too far away! Just west of the most northerly 'Dog Lake' is a wide grassy gully which can be used as a descent to Llyn Llagi. Before thinking about heading down, however, it's well worth exploring the plateau-like expanse to the north where several more pools of various shapes and sizes offer up some excellent compositions.

Viewpoint 7 – Nearly back

From the plateau head WSW taking a gentle downward traverse into the descent gully where Llyn Llagi will come into view. Soon you will meet a path which takes you through an old wall and past a heap of slate spoil. Continue to the next wall through which you can pass by a ruined shepherds hut. The ground now becomes very damp but a keen eye will keep the path underfoot until the next wall is reached. Beyond lies an arcadia of rock outcrops and hawthorns which is not only incredibly pretty but full of photographic subjects. It would be quite easy to spend hours here and the whole area is worthy of a visit in its own right. In the summer months bracken can obscure the path but a watchful approach and the odd waymarker will see you down to a flat marshy area where a stream is crossed twice in quick succession before a polished rocky staircase leads down to a gate/stile combination. In front of a white cottage cross a stile and then go across the field to the next homestead where after a hundred yards you'll meet the Nantmor road. Turn left and follow the road back to your car. The chances are you'll be pretty busy at the computer tonight.

Opposite top left: VP 3. The Cnicht Hotel. *Canon 6D, 24-70mm at 24mm, ISO 100, 1/80 sec at f/8.*

Bottom left: VP 4. The head of Cwm Croesor, Rhosydd Quarry and Moel yr Hydd from Cnicht on a stormy January afternoon. *Canon 6D, 24-70mm at 24mm, ISO 400, 1/60 sec at f/11, 0.6 graduated filter.*

Opposite: VP 7. Craig Llyn Lagi on an April afternoon. *Canon 6D, 24-70mm at 61mm, ISO 100, 1/100 sec at f/11, 0.6 graduated filter.*

Overleaf: VP 5. One of Myriad pools to be found on the Nantmor Skyline backed by Snowdon and the Glyderau. *Canon 7D, 17-40mm at 17mm, ISO 100, 1/6 sec at f/11, tripod, 0.6 graduated filter.*

12 THE MOELWYNION

After driving through the idyllic Lledr Valley and cresting the Crimea Pass your first sight of Blaenau Ffestiniog may come as a bit of a shock. Suddenly you find yourself in a grey world where vast heaps of slate spoil rise skywards, and high hills ravaged by quarrying frown down on narrow streets of closely packed houses, which on rainy days merge into the ashen slopes above. It would be easy to look away in horror until reaching the Vale of Ffestiniog where a more harmonious scene awaits lovers of classical beauty. To do so would be a mistake, as first impressions rarely tell the whole story and high above little 'Blaenau' stand a group of shapely peaks where wild mountain splendour meets post-industrial dereliction, a heady mix that photographers will find irresistible.

Reaching its zenith on the 2530ft summit of Moelwyn Mawr this wonderfully varied walk also visits little brother Moel yr Hydd before exploring the old Rhosydd quarry, a fascinating and deeply affecting place where ghosts of the past, if not seen, can certainly be felt amongst the decaying relics of former glories. The final leg takes you into Cwmorthin, a rewarding photographic location in its own right but on this occasion just one of several attractions to be enjoyed on this splendid journey.

VP 2. Cnicht and the Eifionydd hills from Moelwyn Mawr on a January afternoon. Canon 6D, 24-70mm at 24mm, ISO 100, 1/10 sec at f/11, tripod, 0.6 graduated filter.

12 THE MOELWYNION

The walk

From the parking area turn left and go through the gate which leads to a footbridge. Here you'll find an attractive waterfall which no doubt you'll want to shoot. The walk, however, has just begun, there is a long way still to go and you'll be passing this way again later (when light levels are more conducive to photographing water) so don't feel you have to take action just yet.

Beyond the footbridge the Llyn Stwlan service road is followed beneath Clogwyn Yr Oen on which you're likely to see climbers enjoying their sport on superb slabby rock. After a series of hairpin bends the concrete teeth of Stwlan dam come into view and a signed path on the left is taken which leads to the foot of the dam. Here, a path finds its way up a narrow gash in a rock step to the top of the dam, on the left-hand side of which a passage is made into the boggy environs of the llyn.

Viewpoint 1 – Craigysgafn

To the West lie the two principle Moelwyn peaks (Bach and Mawr respectively) separated by Bwlch Stwlan and the impressive ridge of Craigysgafn. A beeline should be made for the bwlch where a right turn presents a short but 'slippery when wet' scramble onto the ridge and a stunning prospect west down the Dwyryd estuary and over to the Eifionydd hills. Should you wish to include Moelwyn Bach (the summit of which discloses a fine southward view over Llyn Trawsfynydd) a left turn at Bwlch Stwlan where a slatey path gains the summit in around 20 minutes.

VP 5. The Afon Cwmorthin at the end of the day.
Canon 6D, 24-70mm at 42mm, ISO 100, 1.6 sec at f/11, tripod, polarising filter.

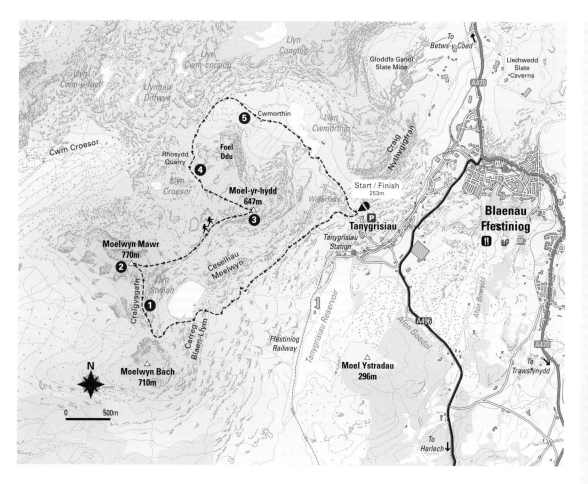

How to get here

The car park stands above the little village of Tanygrisiau a short distance SW of Blaenau Ffestiniog. From the A496 turn onto the road signed Tanygrisiau and then immediately left onto a minor road signed Gorsaf Drydan (Ffestiniog Power Station) and follow it as it climbs to a T-junction. Turn left for the car park.

Parking postcode: LL41 3SW
Parking grid ref: SH 68396 45366
Parking lat/long: 52.988731, -3.962706
Map: OS Explorer Map OL17 (1:25 000) Snowdon / Conwy Valley

Accessibility

This is a moderate hill walk of 6 miles / 9.7km with 746 metres of ascent. Paths range from a reservoir service road and quarry tracks to faint paths which can be boggy especially around Moel yr Hydd and Llyn Stwlan. Under true winter conditions the initial scramble onto Craigysgafn can be tricky and the ascent and descent of Moelwyn Mawr tackle steep slopes where axe and crampon skills are essential.

Best time of year/day

Standing apart from other ranges of hills the Moelwynion gather excellent light year round at both ends of the day. As with all mountain photography days of sunshine and showers make it possible to capture fine images even in the summer months. Peak autumn is the best time to visit with the hills taking on golden tones accentuated by the low angle of the sun.

Overleaf: VP 1. Looking north east over Llyn Stwlan from Moelwyn Bach on an October afternoon. Six shot stitched panorama. Canon 6D, 24-70mm at 24mm, ISO 100, 1/160 sec at f/7.1, 0.9 graduated filter.

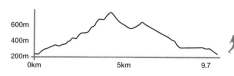

ELEVATION: Lowest: 253m   Highest: 770m   Total ascent: 745.5m
DISTANCE: 6 miles / 9.7 kilometres

12 THE MOELWYNION

Viewpoint 2 – Moelwyn Mawr

Coming up is something not be missed, the finest panorama in Northern Snowdonia. Carry on along Craigysgafn, enjoying every step, before hauling yourself up the steep switch back path onto Moelwyn Mawr's summit dome. The trig point comes into view at the very last second and with it a vista so jaw-droppingly beautiful it will quite literally stop you in your tracks. The view itself is similar to that from Cnicht but more expansive in 360 degrees and with the added bonus of numerous bodies of water large and small to be counted at your leisure. Photographically anything and everything goes here, telephoto, stitched panoramas and 'figures in the landscape' images utilising Mawr's photogenic western ridge. Even the trig pillar is a pretty one and adds foreground interest to wider scenes. It should be noted that in inclement weather Moelwyn Mawr's summit offers no shelter whatsoever.

VP 2. Caroline Barker approaching the summit of Moelwyn Mawr with Moelwyn Bach beyond – January. Canon 6D, 24-70mm at 24mm, ISO 100, 1/30 sec at f/11, 0.9 graduated filter.

12 THE MOELWYNION

Viewpoint 3 – Moel yr Hydd

Upon leaving the summit a few paces east brings a clear path underfoot. This path leads down to Croesor quarry so leave it alone and continue on a rightwards trending descent which joins and follows a fence. Stick with the fence through some spongey territory and then follow the rising path which without too much huff and puff deposits you onto the minor peak of Moel yr Hydd. The Moelwynion are wonderful to look from but also great to look at and this modest little hilltop is as good a place as any from which to photograph their distinctive outline. It is also adorned with some excellent foreground opportunities in the shape of a series of slate flakes which act as strong lead-in lines. Once again this Moelwyn top can be a windy and exposed place with nowhere to hide; but a faint trod heading roughly NE soon takes you down the upper environs of Rhosydd where shelter can be sought behind a dilapidated ruin which proves to be an irresistible foreground subject with Cnicht's unfashionable broadside as the backdrop.

Viewpoint 4 – Rhosydd

So far it's all been about the mountains but now the mood is about to change from exaltation to melancholy as we explore the remains of Rhosydd, all at once a blot on the landscape and a poignant reminder of those that toiled here. The main 'meat' of Rhosydd lies below this windswept plateau and is discovered via a path leading to an incline which is followed down to an abandoned wasteland festooned with rusting junk and buildings in various states of decay. A relatively small area it may be but it is one that will keep you busy for as long as you wish with repeat visits recommended, especially when snow tidies the mess and simplifies compositions.

VP 3. Foel Ddu rising out of the cloud from Moel yr Hydd – February afternoon. Canon 6D, 24-70mm at 57mm, ISO 100, 1/200 sec at f/7.1, 0.6 graduated filter.

VP 4. Rhosydd relics glowing in late February light. Canon 6D, 24-70mm at 24mm, ISO 100, 1/50 sec at f/11, tripod, 0.9 graduated filter.

12 THE MOELWYNION

Viewpoint 5 – Cwmorthin

When the urge to move on grips you a short stroll northwards will bring you to a well-made track descending into Cwmorthin passing a large cascade on the way which, with a bit of ingenuity can be used to hone those long exposures. As the track reaches the bottom of the cwm you'll immediately want to shoot the old barracks. This is also a good place for macro work as the walls are plastered in many varieties of lichen. A little further on a slate fence and the track itself lead the eye beautifully towards an old chapel. This is probably 'the' classic shot of Cwmorthin and can be revisited time and again as the seasons change. Another set of barracks present themselves on your way out of the cwm but do not neglect to have a scout around the water's edge before you leave via a slab bridge which crosses the outflow of the llyn. Before long your car comes into view and just when you thought it was all over there's that waterfall again, the one you walked past at the start of the day. It's well worth a few minutes of anyone's time so go on, fill your boots.

VP 5. The old quarry road wends its way through Cwmorthin – February afternoon. Canon 6D, 24-70mm at 70mm, ISO 100, 0.3 sec at f/11, tripod, 0.6 graduated filter.

13 ARENIG FAWR

Look from the summit of almost any peak in Snowdonia and in the shimmering distance you will see a large camel-backed eminence, aloof in character and exerting territorial dominance over a huge expanse of bleak moorland. That mountain is Arenig Fawr of which George Borrow wrote in his fascinating 1862 travelogue 'Wild Wales'.

"Of all the hills I saw in Wales none made a greater impression upon me".

The big 'Arenig' has many tales to tell, all of them deeply affecting and the air thereabouts is charged with sadness and a pervasive sense of melancholy. What better place to delve into wild Wales, with camera in hand, to commune with the phantoms of yesteryear?

On this north – south traverse Arenig Fawr gives up its secrets one by one and combines wild mountain solitude with a human dimension which affords great opportunities for photographic story telling. Along the way, you'll enjoy one of the most extensive panoramas in the land, learn the tragic tale of young lives cut short and contemplate the loss of a way of life in this neglected mountain sanctuary. This is a walk on which to immerse yourself in the prevailing atmosphere and create images full of pathos and poignancy.

VP 2. A March evening on Craig yr Hyrddod with Arenig Fawr,
Moel Llyfnant and Cadair Idris beyond.
Canon 6D, 24-70mm at 24mm, ISO 100, 1/15 sec at
f/11, 0.6 graduated filter, tripod.

13 ARENIG FAWR

The walk

The site of the old Arenig station is the starting point of the walk and a left turn out of the car park takes you down through a hamlet of the same name. It's a peculiar little place where pylons march across the landscape and a disparate collection of homesteads lie at intervals along the road.

Of all the times I have walked this way I have never seen another person but have often met the goats and barking dogs which reside here. After one-and-a-half-kilometres a gate on the right leads to a wide track which climbs steadily towards the mountain. Before you proceed, take some time to consider that beautiful lake in the valley below.

Viewpoint 1 – Reflection

Llyn Celyn was created in 1965 to slake Liverpool's thirst, a contentious act which over 50 years later still arouses deep resentment. The village of Capel Celyn and the homes of 48 people along with the post office, school and chapel were drowned by the rising waters. Cofiwch Drweryn – Remember Trweryn.

Before long the track levels out on a heathery moor and Llyn Arenig Fawr slides into view beneath a wall of steep crags in a scene that is reminiscent of the Southern Uplands of Scotland. The llyn can be successfully photographed from a distance or from its shore.

VP 1. Bothy Life – Nick Matthews and Dave Dear taking time out in the Llyn Arenig Fawr hut.
Canon 6D, 24-70mm at 24mm, ISO 400, 1/80 sec at f/7.1.

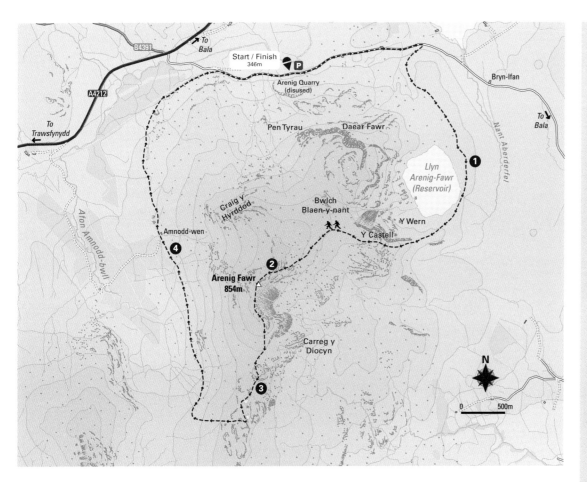

The parking area is 16 miles from Bala and 13.5 miles from Trawsfynydd and is located opposite the large disused quarry on the minor road off the A4212 (signed Arenig, Llidiardau, Rhyd Uchaf, Parc).

Parking postcode: LL23 7PA
Parking grid ref: SH 83017 39225
Parking lat/long: 52.936317, -3.740947
Map: OS Explorer Map OL 18 (1:25 000) Harlech, Porthmadog & Bala/Y Bala

Accessibility

This is a moderate hill walk of 8.7 miles / 14km with 760 metres of ascent. The paths range from well-made access tracks to vague and sketchy between Y Castell and the summit ridge where competent navigation is required in poor visibility. The south ridge and a short stretch beyond Amnodd Wen can be very wet underfoot; gaiters will ensure you remain dry-shod. Sitting further east than the main Snowdonia ranges Arenig Fawr gathers snow more often and in winter conditions the usual caveats apply regarding equipment and experience.

Best time of year/day

Owing to its north-south configuration and not being overlooked by higher mountains Arenig Fawr is a viable proposition for year-round golden hour light at each end of the day. Llyn Arenig Fawr is excellent for sunrise with Craig y Hyrddod and the south ridge best for sunset.

ELEVATION: Lowest: 346m Highest: 854m Total ascent: 760.2m
DISTANCE: 8.7 miles / 14 kilometres

VP 1. Llyn Arenig Fawr on a December morning. Six shot stitched panorama. Canon 6D, 24-70mm at 24mm, ISO 100, 1/80 sec at f/8.

13 ARENIG FAWR

Viewpoint 2 – Llyn Arenig Fawr and Arenig Fawr

Beside the llyn's outflow you'll find one of a handful of Welsh bothies which provides welcome shelter from the elements or a cosy (if a little cramped) haven in which to spend the night. Behind the bothy a stile leads to the outflow which is crossed by an amusing metal ladder. A peaty path now mounts the ridge and the view opens up beautifully with the llyn below ripe for panoramic images. At the top of the ridge carefully cross a fence and then a little further on another on your right where stones have been piled to aid progress. Now to head for the summit.

A faint path heads towards the bulky mass of Arenig Fawr crossing damp ground on the way before striking a rising leftward traverse which after 140 metres of ascent arrives on the summit ridge. Old fence posts here can be used to enhance your compositions and a detour north to Craig y Hyrddod is recommended for a good view across to the summit.

On the summit itself (aka Moel y Eglwys, Bare hill of the church) you can, weather permitting, experience one of the most arresting sights in Snowdonia. It was here in the early hours of August 4th 1943 that an American B17 Flying Fortress crashed killing all on board. There is a memorial plaque in the summit shelter along with fragments of wreckage. Spare a thought for eight young men who perished so very far from home.

As engaging as the vista from Arenig Fawr is, it is difficult to photograph effectively as the surrounding ranges lie many miles away. What comes next, however, makes up for it.

Viewpoint 3 – Arenig Fawr South Ridge

Descend south and then make the short climb onto Arenig Fawr's 'south top'. Below you will see a broad ridge of rocky knolls and small pools. Follow the fence down and start exploring. This whole area feels wonderfully remote and is an absolute joy to wander around. Water features and an old wall aid composition with Arenig's south top taking centre stage and looking every inch a fine mountain.

VP 2. Aproaching the summit on a beautiful February morning. Canon 7D, 17-40mm at 25mm, ISO 320, 1/500 sec at f/11.

VP 2. The Flying Fortress monument on the Summit of Arenig Fawr – March. Canon 6D, 24-70mm at 24mm, ISO 400, 1/50 sec at f/16.

Above: *VP 2. Fragments – Arenig Fawr.*
Canon 6D, 24-70mm at 27mm, ISO 100,
1/30 sec at f/8.

Above left: *VP 2. Moel Lyfnant from*
Arenig fawr South Top – March.
Canon 6D, 24-70mm at 50mm, ISO 100, 1/100
sec at f/11, 0.9 graduated filter, tripod.

VP 2. Heading down to the South Ridge
on a moody March afternoon.
Canon 6D, 24-70mm at 24mm, ISO 100,
1/40 sec at f/11, 0.9 graduated filter, tripod.

VP 3. A March afternoon and Arenig Fawr's south ridge. Canon 6D, 24-70mm at 24mm, ISO 100, 1/20 sec at f/11, polarising filter, 0.6 graduated filter, tripod.

13 ARENIG FAWR

Viewpoint 4 – Amnodd Wen

From the southernmost of the larger pools (close to point 695 on the map) descend a short distance west to a fence crossing and then continue down aiming slightly rightwards for a dilapidated wall over which access to a good track is gained. Once again you are in a quiet, lonely place where you are unlikely to see another soul. Drink in the solitude and imagine what it would have been like to live here before the advent of electricity and other modern creature comforts. The track is pleasant though uneventful until after 2km you come upon a large ruinous settlement.

Amnodd Wen was once the hub of a thriving farming community and inhabited as recently as the 1930s, so I was told one morning by a local farmer I met on Craig y Hyrddod. Nowadays it stands silent and forlorn but is an irresistible photographic subject which comes into its own from late afternoon onwards. As you investigate the possibilities of this evocative location it's difficult not ponder on old ways and the nature of transience. A fitting place, then, to leave a mountain where loss is a recurring theme.

From the ruins follow the track taking the right-hand fork which soon becomes wet underfoot for 700 metres. After a stile the track firms up and continues past an old quarry before re-joining the road which runs adjacent to disused railway line all the way back to your car.

VP 4. The ruins of Amnodd Wen catch the last glimmer of a March evening.
Canon 6D, 24-70mm at 41mm, ISO 100, 0.5 sec at f/11,
0.6 graduated filter, tripod.

14 RHINOG FAWR AND THE CELTIC BADLANDS

Deserted and desolate, feared and forsaken, the Rhinogydd are the closest approximation of an authentic mountain wilderness that Wales has to offer. Tales of waist-deep heather, leg-breaking boulders and man-eating crevices keep the masses at bay but hint at quietude and space on mountains which are as enigmatic as they are remote. Perhaps, then, for every thousand hillgoers put off by such grave warnings there will be one who, while gripped by the spirit of adventure, goes forth into this inviolable area and comes out the other side enthralled. When asked about their day they usually become taciturn, muttering vague, expletive-riddled oaths in the hope that the Rhinogydd remain inviolate to all but world-weary misanthropes, feral goats and epicures of esoterica; they have found somewhere very special indeed, and want to keep it to themselves. And so, over time, the myths persist …

If hill walkers are thin on the ground around these parts then photographers are fewer still and have yet to infiltrate a landscape which has more in common with Scotland's North West than the Snowdonia most of us know and love. Gritstone pavements littered with glacial erratics, deep-cut canyons and hidden lakes provide plenty of subject matter to work with. However, the real challenge, should you choose to accept it, is to tap into the primeval atmosphere and inject some of it into your images.

VP 2. Jamie Rooke toasting the Summer Solstice on Craig Wion with Llyn Morwynion below and the Lleyn Peninsular beyond. Canon 6D, 24-70mm at 31mm, ISO 100, 1/30 sec at f/11, 0.9 graduated filter, tripod.

14 RHINOG FAWR AND THE CELTIC BADLANDS

The walk

Turn right out of the car park and just past the first farm building go left through two gates (signed 'To Clip'). After entering a small field enclosure trend rightwards and go over a break in the wall.

The path is little more than a sheep trod and in summer the way ahead is concealed by thick bracken. The best course of action is to mount the tilted rock outcrops on the left as soon as possible.

Viewpoint 1 – Cwm Bychan

You haven't been walking for long but already the view across to Rhinog Fawr and over Llyn Cwm Bychan is stunning and well worth spending some time with. This is a scene that greatly benefits from late light especially in late summer when the valley and the many gritstone terraces are side-lit revealing all the texture within this contorted landscape. A better path is intercepted as you gain height and crosses a stile, rising gently through heather and across a flat, boggy area before reaching another stile at Bwlch Gwylim.

How to get here

The key to Cwm Bychan is the little village of Llanbedr which is on the A496 coast road 3.2 miles from Harlech and 7.4 miles from Barmouth. At the Victoria Inn turn left or right depending on your direction of approach and follow the road (ignoring the right turn to Cwm Nantcol) all the way to the parking area in Cwm Bychan (honesty box for parking fees). From Pentre Gwynfryn the road is single track for about 5 miles with various passing places and care should be taken as high walls obscure distant views and livestock of various species often wander onto the road from nearby farmsteads. At certain times of the year there will be gates that need to be opened, be sure to close them again on your way through.

Parking postcode: LL45 2PH
Parking grid ref: SH 64567 31459
Parking lat/long: 52.865405, -4.012874
Map: OS Explorer Map OL18 (1:25 000)
Harlech, Porthmadog & Bala/Y Bala

Accessibility

This is a strenuous mountain walk of 7.4 miles / 12km with 1010 metres of ascent. Apart from the Roman Steps, which are excellent, the paths throughout this walk range from serviceable to vague, when vigilance and mountain sense should be employed. If exploring 'off piste' be sure to return to the nearest path to continue your journey especially if snow is present; free-range heather bashing in the Rhinogydd should not be underestimated in terms of difficulty, exasperation and sheer misery.

VP 1. Rhinog Fawr from above Cwm Bychan on an August afternoon. Canon 6D, 24-70mm at 50mm, ISO 100, 1/60 sec at f/8, tripod, 0.9 graduated filter.

Opposite: VP 7. Spring folliage on the Roman Steps path to Cwm Bychan – May. Canon 6D, 24-70mm at 24mm, ISO 100, 1/80 sec at f/11, 0.9 graduated filter.

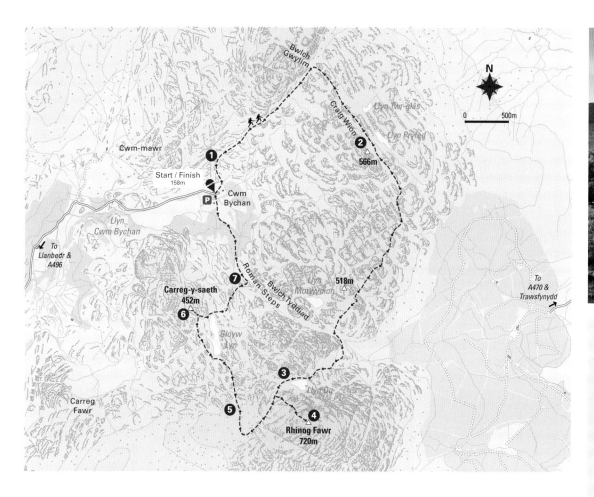

Start / Finish
158m

Cwm-mawr

Cwm
Bychan

Llyn
Cwm Bychan

To
Llanbedr &
A496

Bwlch
Gwylim

Craig Wron

Llyn Twr-glas

Llyn Pryfed

2
566m

Roman Steps

Bwlch
Tyddiad

Llyn
Morwynion

518m

To
A470 &
Trawsfynydd

7

Carreg-y-saeth
452m

6

Gloyw
Lyn

Carreg
Fawr

3

Llyn Du

5

4

Rhinog Fawr
720m

N

0   500m

600m
400m
200m

0km   5km   10km   12km

ELEVATION: Lowest: 158m   Highest: 720m   Total ascent: 1011.7m
DISTANCE: 7.4 miles / 12 kilometres

Best time of year/day

The Rhinogydd's north-south alignment ensure great morning and evening light year-round. Aside from the golden hours, the Rhinogydd, being largely heather-clad can appear quite drab with uniform brown slopes for much of the year. Cwm Bychan and the lower part of the Roman Steps are at their best in spring and autumn when the ancient woodland displays wonderful colouring. Higher up, late summer sees the mountains awash with purples and violets along with the vivid yellow of gorse bushes. Their proximity to the sea means that full winter conditions are rarer – though not unheard of – than on the high mountains further north. When such conditions prevail the utmost caution is required and the full round can only be recommended to strong walkers with prior knowledge of the route.

Viewpoint 2 – Craig Wion and the Rhinogydd Canyonlands

Turn right and climb out of the bwlch to access Craig Wion, a broad ridge of peaty moorland interspersed with small gritstone pavements. A faint path of sorts meanders in and out of damp patches and stays within spitting distance of a beautifully constructed stone wall. Where a low crag appears to bar your way, a weakness facilitates progress and soon you come upon the first of two cairned tops. The view is remarkable and the ambience prehistoric. Erratics are strewn around and compositions can be found everywhere. Further on, a higher top can be gained by carefully scrambling onto the summit plinth from either side of the wall. Llyn Pryfed lies to your left in a sunken trough and to the south Rhinog Fawr rears up, looking further away than it really is. In between you and the sanctuary of Bwlch Tyddiad lies what Harold Drasdo described in the classic 'Wild Walks' book as "a splendid mile of celtic badlands". Gird your loins for some rough stuff!

From the cairn, follow the line of least resistance in a south easterly direction down to a grassy depression. Here, the way ahead 'dog-legs' to the south west. Crest the high point of the ridge where a path can be found and with a little vigilance followed through the 'Rhinogydd Canyonlands'. There are four transverse canyons which carve their way through the ridge and it is important to find the correct way into and out of them by using signs of traffic and the lie of the land to guide you through a maze of crag and boulder. The canyons themselves are not particularly photogenic but in negotiating them the sense of adventure and isolation should be savoured for this is as 'out there' as Snowdonia gets. Towards the end of the traverse huge pavements of Cambrian gritstone, cracked and scoured by ice, will stop you in your tracks. Time to get the camera out! Before descending to Bwlch Tyddiad it is well worth the short detour west to the spot height of 458 where Llyn Morwynion can be viewed in all its secluded glory. From here you can look back on the first half of your journey and wonder how you survived the experience. For those with little fuel left in the tank a right turn at Bwlch Tyddiad will see you back at the start in less than an hour making it perfectly feasible to split the route in two. For everyone else, however …

VP 2. Rhinog Fawr looming above Bwlch Tyddiad on an August afternoon. Canon 6D, 24-70mm at 33mm, ISO 100, 0.3 sec at f/16, tripod, polarising filter, 0.9 graduated filter.

VP 2. Rhinog Fawr stands beyond the celtic badlands of Craig Wion on a March afternoon. Canon 6D, 24-70mm at 24mm, ISO 100, 1/100 sec at f/11, tripod, 0.6 and 0.9 graduated filters.

VP 2. Glacial erratics on Craig Wion – November. Canon 7D, 17-40mm at 17mm, ISO 100, 1/15 sec at f/11, tripod, 0.6 graduated filter.

VP 3. The dark waters of Llyn Du on an October afternoon. Canon 6D, 24-70mm at 32mm, ISO 100, 1/80 sec at f/11, polarising filter, 0.9 graduated filter.

14 RHINOG FAWR AND THE CELTIC BADLANDS

Viewpoint 3 – Llyn Du

Bwlch Tyddiad marks the high point of the 'Roman Steps' which, rather than being
the handy work of 'Claudius and the gang' are thought to form part of a medieval
packhorse route. From the bwlch descend SW a short distance (if you find yourself at the
information board you have gone too far) and pick up a narrow peaty path in the best
Rhinog tradition which curves around to the right and climbs steadily through heather
and then across boulders to find Llyn Du (the Black Lake) nestling beneath Rhinog Fawr's
impressive north face and quite living up to its name. The dark waters of the llyn are
rarely still and lake-side compositions are tricky but with a bit of perseverance and a
polarising filter it is possible to capture the mood of this wild, lonely location.

Viewpoint 4 – Rhinog Fawr

From the outflow of the llyn pick your way across its bouldery northern shore and follow
the path to a wall. Turn left and follow the wall crossing over a break where it meets a
steep crag and takes a right-angle turn. Continue for a short distance keeping an eye
out on the left for a path which winds its way through heather and rock before striking
up steep scree to the summit of Rhinog Fawr. The scene that awaits you is breathtaking.
Photographically your best bet is to head southwards across the summit plateau for
shots over Bwlch Drws Ardudwy to Rhinog Fach and Y Llethr. Side lighting either early
of late in the day really brings this landscape to life but do take some time to explore
the surrounding area for compositional options.

Viewpoint 5 – Towards Gloywlyn

There are several paths which descend from Rhinog Fawr but without experience of their
serpentine ways it is perhaps best to go down the way you came and return to the wall.
That done, turn left and follow the path which more or less follows the wall until reaching
a gate. Beyond the gate you find yourself on an extensive moor and the path, counter
intuitively, heads in completely the wrong direction. However, stick with it as a direct line

towards Gloywlyn is more trouble than it's worth. After around 250 metres look out for another path which cuts in from the right. Although intermittent, this route will eventually funnel you down a gully and beside a stream, from the top of which Gloywlyn – one of Snowdonia's most exquisite hidden gems – bursts into view. With some careful scouting off the beaten track you can find some superb compositions on ground which looks like it's never felt the tread of human feet let alone those of a tripod. Back in the gully, go through a break in the wall and follow the stream down to Gloywlyn where the stream itself can be used as a terrific leading line which threads its way through blonde grasses to Carreg y Saeth. On a clear day, Snowdon is framed beautifully in the gap at the end of the lake.

VP 4. Rhinog Fach and Y Llethr from Rhinog Fawr on a March afternoon. Canon 7D, 17-40mm at 17mm, ISO 100, 1/30 sec at f/11, tripod, 0.9 graduated filter.

VP 5. Gloywlyn and Carreg y Saeth on a March evening. Canon 7D, 17-40mm at 17mm, ISO 100, 1/8 sec at f/11, tripod, 0.6 graduated filter.

VP 6. Gloywlyn and Rhinog Fawr from Carreg y Saeth on a capricious April afternoon. Canon 6D, 24-70mm at 24mm, ISO 100, 1/80 sec at f/11, tripod, 0.9 graduated filter.

VP 7. Gloywlyn and Carreg y Saeth on an August afternoon. Canon 6D, 24-70mm at 24mm, ISO 100, ¼ sec at f/22, tripod, 0.9 graduated filter.

VP 6. Helen Iles gazing across Gloywlyn to Rhinog Fawr from Carreg y Saeth on a July evening. Canon 6D, 24-70mm at 24mm, ISO 100, 1/10 sec at f/11, tripod, 0.6 graduated filter.

Four shot stiched panorama.

14 RHINOG FAWR AND THE CELTIC BADLANDS

Viewpoint 6 – Carreg y Saeth

At this stage in the game an ascent of Carreg y Saeth might be seen as an added extra to what has already been a full day but the short pathless climb shouldn't be missed for the tremendous panorama it affords. Traverse around Gloywlyn's western shore and near the northern tip of the lake weave a way through heather, bilberry and broken rock up onto the shoulder of the hill for bird's eye view of Gloywlyn and Rhinog Fawr beyond. Bear in mind that it's not necessary to climb to Carreg y Saeth's summit for the most compelling perspective. Indeed, from the top of the hill you'll find that Gloywlyn has vanished and with it a very satisfying visual element which you will almost certainly want to include in your images.

Viewpoint 7 – Roman Steps

Slowly retrace your steps to Gloywlyn's northern extremity, mount the slab-walled low relief ridge which runs along its eastern margin and pick up a path which takes a circuitous route through the usual mix of peat and heather. Before long good views of Cwm Bychan and Clip open up which, on late summer evenings attract any available light. Carry on across a stream until meeting a stile beyond which two paths present themselves. Take the one which bears right to join the Roman Steps. Here, on this unkempt and heavily vegetated thoroughfare you'll find image making opportunities galore; an old packhorse bridge, lone hawthorn trees and the sinuous line of the 'Steps' themselves which form an irresistible leading line in both directions. After crossing the packhorse bridge you will enter ancient woodland which will enchant you through all four seasons. A stile leads to a walled cart track which spans a stream before an iron gate on the left delivers you back to your car. During this final chapter of the day you may realise that all the most photogenic locations can be accessed individually and with relatively little effort by using the Roman Steps/Bwlch Tyddiad and the initial approach to Craig Wion which opens up the possibility of satisfying bite-sized outings for when time is short; worth considering as no doubt you will have fallen under the spell of this timeless and rewarding landscape. There is nowhere quite like the Rhinogydd.

VP 7. Cwm Bychan and Clip on an August evening. Canon 6D, 24-70mm at 24mm, ¼ sec at f/11, tripod, 0.6 and 0.9 graduated filters.

VP 7. Clip rising above Cwm Bychan on an October afternoon. Canon 6D, 24-70mm at 28mm, ISO 100, 1/200 sec at f/8, 0.9 graduated filter.

15 CADAIR IDRIS

Taking the form of a seven-mile long escarpment Cadair Idris' regal skyline soars above the Mawddach estuary in one last expression of volcanic cragginess before the mountains of the north give way to the smooth contours of mid Wales. Although the national park boundary lies some twelve miles distant, Cadair marks the true southern frontier of Snowdonia and is without any shadow of a doubt one of its most photographically rewarding ranges. Folklore tells us that in the distant past it was the haunt of 'Idris', a giant who wrote poetry and studied the stars from this lofty chair (cadair in Welsh) and more recently an old hag sold sandwiches and lemonade from a rude hut on the summit.

Nowadays the only giant hereabouts is the mountain itself and you'll have to carry up your own lemonade but this hasn't made Cadair any less popular. The Minffordd Path continues to be one of the busiest in the land and a splendid introduction to the mountain. However, this route which tackles the Fox's Path is a quieter, stiffer and an aesthetically more rewarding expedition offering the hill walking photographer a feast of scenic delights which unfold one after the other.

Kris Williams greets the dawn on Cadair Idris after a chilly wildcamp in March. Four shot stitched panorama. Canon 6D, 24-70mm at 24mm, ISO 100, 1/4 sec at f/11, 0.9 graduated filter, tripod.

15 CADAIR IDRIS

The walk

Leaving the car park can be a wrench as its babbling stream and picnic tables provide an almost irresistible inducement to linger, but leave it you must for the day is young and there is much to see and photograph.

Ignoring a large sign to the contrary, turn left and walk for about a kilometre along the road in idyllic surroundings until the whitewashed Gwernan Lake Hotel throws up another potential derailment of your progress. Directly opposite is a gate through which you are ushered away from lesser temptations and delivered onto a path which becomes more enchanting with every step.

Viewpoint 1 – The Lower Fox's Path

Before long you are above the valley and can peer down on a vision of verdant beauty which would not be out of place in the Lake District. Ahead of you the mighty northern wall of Cadair rears up and all around are secretive dells and gnarled hawthorns demanding your photographic attention. Leaving the trodden ways to explore shaded corners, hillocks and knolls can be a very profitable exercise in terms of discovering hidden gems and seldom seen compositions.

Top: VP 1. Cadair's northern crags come into view on a beautiful April afternoon. Canon 7D, 17-40mm at 17mm, ISO 100, 1/50 sec at f/11, 0.6 graduated filter.
Bottom: VP 1. Looking towards Bryn Brith at the end of a September day on the Fox's Path. Canon 7D, 17-40mm at 17mm, ISO 100, 0.5 sec at f/11, 0.6 and 0.9 graduated filters, tripod.

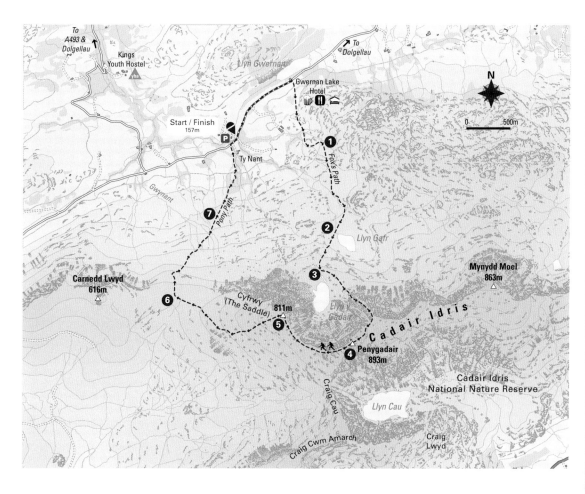

ELEVATION: Lowest: 157m   Highest: 893m   Total ascent: 817.4m
DISTANCE: 5.7 miles / 9.3 kilometres

How to get here

From the A470 turn onto the A493 signed Tywyn and then take the next left signed Dolgellau. After 0.8 miles and directly opposite Penbryn Garage take a sharp right hand turn and follow the road for about two and a half miles before reaching the car park at Ty Nant.

Parking postcode: LL40 1TN
Parking grid ref: SH 69788 15274
Parking lat/long: 52.719459, -3.929285
Map: OS Explorer Map OL23 (1:25 000) Cadair Idris and Llyn Tegid

Accessibility

This is a moderately challenging high mountain walk of 5.7 miles / 9.3km with 817 metres of ascent. The paths are clear and easy to follow although a short passage on the screes of the upper Fox's Path requires care and a steady approach. If you are inexperienced on or daunted by loose terrain then a contouring path from Cwm Gadair can be followed to where it joins the Pony Path at SH 69146 13743 from where an 'an out and back' ascent of Pen y Gadair can be easily achieved at the cost of a few extra kilometres.

Best time of year/day

Cadair's east/west alignment makes it a great location for year-round golden hour light at both ends of the day. The northern facet of the mountain remains in shadow for much of the year but is struck by evening light from early April to late August. In winter conditions the usual caveats apply regarding the use of ice axe and crampons with the Fox's screes being a potential problem for the inexperienced. Under snow and ice the walk can be made relatively safe by taking a diversion onto the Pony Path from Cwm Gadair.

15 CADAIR IDRIS

Viewpoint 2 – Llyn Gafr

The path eventually passes through a gate which signals change. Cadair still remains as the backdrop but lush pastures have been replaced by an austere landscape of damp moorland redolent of another altogether wilder realm, that of a great giant perhaps. Your way crosses two streams and then, without warning, you find yourself beside Llyn Gafr, the 'Goat Lake'. On a late summer evening when the heather is in bloom this placid body of water is an uplifting location, Scottish in character and with the ambience of a great glaciated wilderness.

Viewpoint 3 – Cwm Gadair

From Llyn Gafr the route forges upwards on a well cairned path which takes you to one of the most arresting spectacles in the Welsh mountains, Cwm Gadair. Here you'll find a secluded lake, above which, rising in tiered steeps is Pen y Gadair, your eventual high point of the day. To its right and from vast fans of scree the awesome Cyfrwy Arete thrusts skywards and has for over a hundred years thrown down a challenge that few climbers can resist. For the adventurous photographer however the upper Fox's path will provided plenty of excitement but before we get there let's look at what to point our cameras at. The water's edge is the obvious place to start and a polarising filter can be used to reveal its bouldery depths. Climbing onto the moraine affords a wider perspective of the llyn while further west and onto the lower screes brings the north facing Cyfrwy Arete into profile which in the months of spring and summer is kissed by late evening light.

VP 1. The first signs of autumn on the Foxes path – September evening.
Two shot stitched panorama. Canon 7D, 17-40mm at 17mm,
ISO 100, 0.5 sec at f/11, 0.9 graduated filter, tripod.

VP 2. Heather in bloom beside Llyn Gafr on an Early September evening. Four shot stitched panorama. Canon 7D, 17-40mm at 17mm, ISO 100, 1/6 sec at f/11, 0.9 graduated filter, tripod.

VP 3. Cyfrwy and an inquisitive inhabitant of Cwm Gadair on a September afternoon. Canon 7D, 17-40mm at 17mm, ISO 100, 1/50 sec at f/11, 0.6 and 0.9 graduated filters.

15 CADAIR IDRIS

Viewpoint 4 – Pen y Gadair

Back at the llyn the final ascent to Pen y Gadair is grimly apparent. A prolonged grind up the centre of the ridge has, over the years, become run-out, insecure underfoot and rather unpleasant. A much safer way, although still with a measure of loose terrain, is to walk over to the toe of the ridge and carefully tackle the leftmost patch of light coloured scree which, after a brief slitherfest, brings you onto firmer ground and a developing path which improves all the way up onto the summit plateau. Pen y Gadair's top is just five minutes away and its palatial refuge hut is a welcome sight in wet or windy weather.

The panorama on a clear day is extensive, ranging from Pen y Fan in the south to Carnedd Llewelyn in the north, but the most striking images home in on more intimate views. A short descent SE discloses Llyn Cau, far below and hemmed in by the steep crags of Craig Cau. Rather than settling for the first thing you find here, it is worth scouting around the outcrops upon which foreground interest is abundant. Back on the summit and perched on the edge of Cwm Gadair there awaits an extraordinary scene across Llyn y Gadair to Cyfrwy and the glittering sea beyond. If climbers happen to be on the Cyfrwy Arete then telephoto shots can work really well in conveying the true scale of the mountain.

Viewpoint 5 – Cyfrwy

From the summit hut follow the rim of the cwm all the way round to the stony top of Cyfrwy, a Cinderella peak often missed by folk hurrying down the Pony Path but a grand spot from which to survey your ascent as well as Cadair's eastern continuation over Mynydd Moel and farther afield to Rhobell Fawr, the Arennigs and Aran Fawddwy. Of an evening this is a superlative viewpoint and one that can be savoured safe in the knowledge that your descent route is uncomplicated and free from difficulties under torchlight should you wish to remain until the final curtain.

VP 3. Llyn y Gadair on a fine April afternoon. Canon 6D, 24-70mm at 29mm, ISO 100, 1/15 sec at f/11, circular polarising filter, 0.6 and 0.9 graduated filters, tripod.

Viewpoint 6 – The Pony Path

The homeward leg may lack the drama of the first half of the day but there is still plenty of inspiration to be had from the gentler settings you'll encounter on the way down. From Cyfrwy a course SW will bring you onto the Pony Path, a veritable motor way which whisks you down to the crossroads of Rhiw Gwredydd where a tumbledown wall invites a photographic study in leading lines as it snakes upwards towards Cyfrwy. Onwards and after taking the second of two adjacent gates you're almost done but here, as on the lower Fox's Path, there are trees to be enjoyed. Some are stunted, others withered but all are full of character and hanging on for dear life from the constant onslaught of prevailing westerlies. Get to know them a little before following the waymarked trail back to the road where a right turn sees you back at your car in no time at all. In the gloaming the atmosphere of the valley is as peaceful and romantic as can be, a salubrious end to a memorable day.

VP 3. Digby Tilton indulging in some optional scrambling on the Fox's Path high above Llyn Gafr.
Canon 6D, 24-70mm at 30mm, ISO 100, 1/160 sec at f/8, 0.6 graduated filter.

VP 5. The last colours of a May evening catch the top of Mynydd Moel from Cyfrwy. Canon 6D, 24-70mm at 24mm, ISO 100, 0.4 sec at f/11, 0.9 graduated filter, tripod.

Opposite*: VP 4. Looking across Cwm Gadair to Cyfrwy on a hazy day in May.* Canon 6D, 24-70mm at 24mm, ISO 100, 1/400 sec at f/11, 0.6 and 0.9 graduated filters, tripod.

VP 6. Cyfrwy from Rhiw Gwredydd on an April evening. Canon 6D, 24-70mm at 26mm, ISO 100, 1/160 sec at f/8, 0.6 graduated filter.

Overleaf*: VP 4. Three walkers heading to Mynydd Moel from the top of the Fox's Path – February afternoon.* Canon 6D, 24-70mm at 24mm, ISO 100, 1/30 sec at f/11, 0.9 graduated filter.

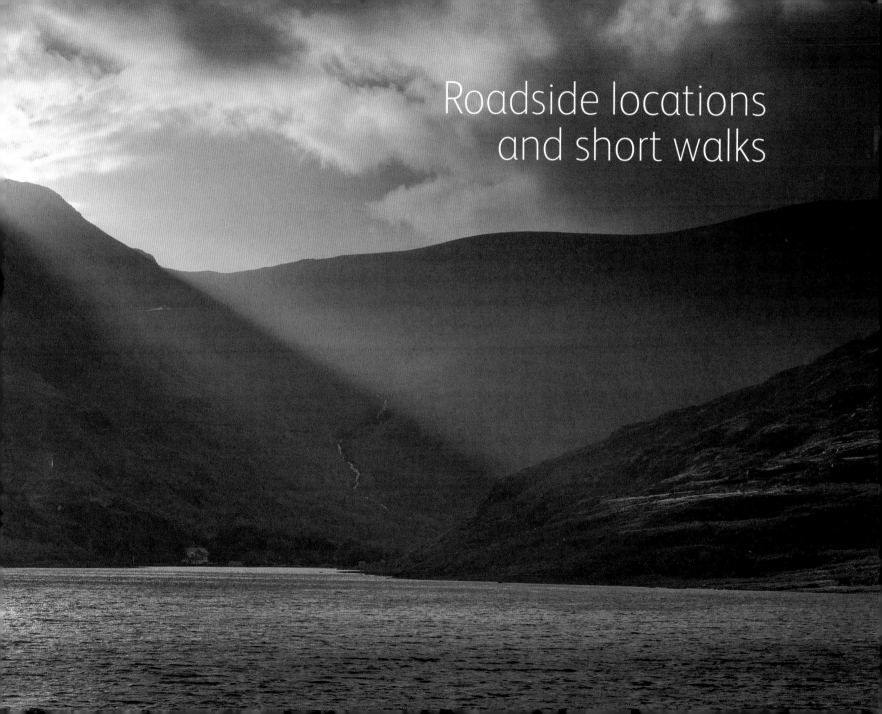

Roadside locations
and short walks

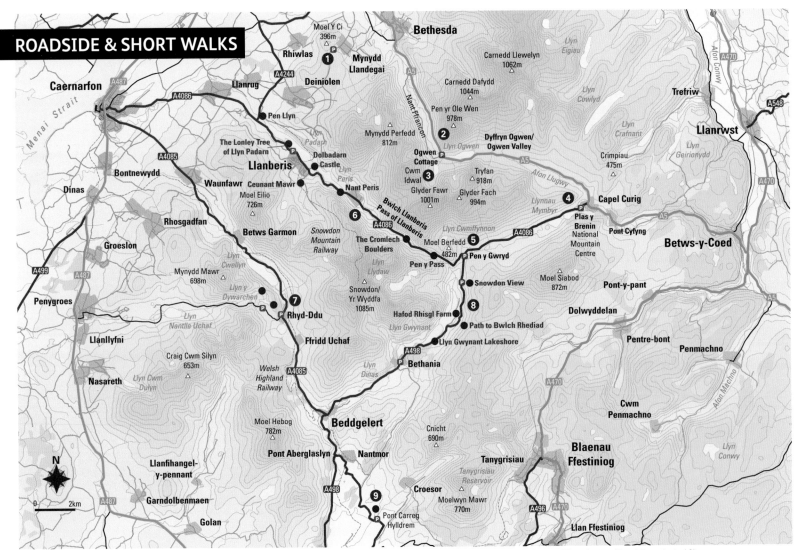

ROADSIDE & SHORT WALKS

Moel Y Ci
396m

Rhiwlas

1

Mynydd
Llandegai

Bethesda

Carnedd Llewelyn
1062m

Llyn
Eigiau

Caernarfon

Deiniolen

Carnedd Dafydd
1044m

Trefriw

Llanrug

A4244

A5

Nant Ffrancon

Pen yr Ole Wen
978m

Llyn
Cowlyd

Pen Llyn

A4086

Mynydd Perfedd
812m

2

Dyffryn Ogwen/
Ogwen Valley

Llyn
Crafnant

Llanrwst

Llyn
Padarn

Ogwen
Cottage

Llyn Ogwen

Afon Llugwy

Crimpiau
475m

Llyn
Geirionydd

The Lonley Tree
of Llyn Padarn

Dolbadarn
Castle

Cwm
Idwal

3

Tryfan
918m

Llanberis

Llyn
Peris

Ceunant Mawr

Nant Peris

Glyder Fawr
1001m

Glyder Fach
994m

Capel Curig

4

Waunfawr

Moel Eilio
726m

Bwlch Llanberis
Pass of Llanberis

Llynnau
Mymbyr

Plas y
Brenin
National
Mountain
Centre

Pont Cyfyng

A5

Bontnewydd

Dinas

Betws Garmon

6

A4086

Moel Berfedd
482m

Llyn Cwmffynnon

A4086

5

Pen y Gwryd

Betws-y-Coed

Rhosgadfan

Snowdon
Mountain
Railway

The Cromlech
Boulders

Pen y Pass

Groeslon

Mynydd Mawr
698m

Llyn
Cwellyn

Llyn
Llydaw

Moel Siabod
872m

Pont-y-pant

A499

A487

Llyn y
Dywarchen

7

Snowdon/
Yr Wyddfa
1085m

Snowdon View

8

Dolwyddelan

Penygroes

Rhyd-Ddu

Hafod Rhisgl Farm

Path to Bwlch Rhediad

Llanllyfni

Ffridd Uchaf

Llyn Gwynant

Llyn Gwynant Lakeshore

Pentre-bont

Penmachno

Craig Cwm Silyn
653m

Welsh
Highland
Railway

A498

Bethania

A4085

Llyn
Dinas

Nasareth

Llyn Cwm
Dulyn

A470

**Cwm
Penmachno**

Moel Hebog
782m

Beddgelert

Cnicht
690m

**Blaenau
Ffestiniog**

Llyn
Conwy

N

Pont Aberglaslyn

Nantmor

Tanygrisiau

**Llanfihangel-
y-pennant**

Tanygrisiau
Reservoir

A487

0   2km

A498

9

Croesor

Moelwyn Mawr
770m

A496

A470

Garndolbenmaen

Pont Carreg
Hylldrem

Golan

Llan Ffestiniog

Previous spread: Crespuscular rays over Y Garn from Llyn Ogwen on a September afternoon. Canon 6D, 24-70mm at 44mm, ISO 100, 1/200 sec at f/8, polarising filter, 1.5 graduated filter.

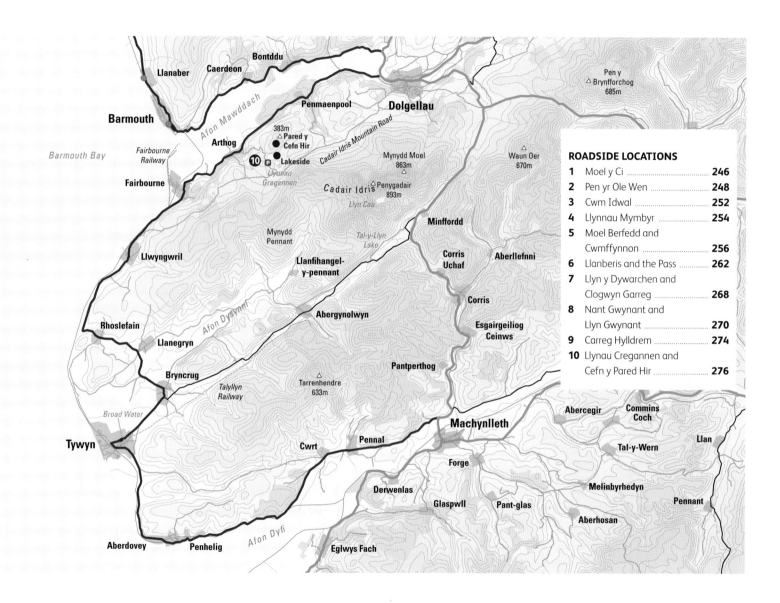

ROADSIDE LOCATIONS

01 MOEL Y CI

Moel y Ci is a little gem of a hill known only to the most ardent of hillbaggers and the people of Rhiwlas and Mynydd Llandegai for whom it is a constant presence in their day to day lives. There are no towering crags or slender ridges hereabouts, only a heather clad moorland plateau peppered with a rash of beautiful pale rocks. As an object in itself Moel y Ci is quite unremarkable which might explain why it is off the radar of virtually every photographer visiting Snowdonia. However, for those in the know it is a coveted location and one from which to snatch a few images at the end of a day when the weather or time has conspired against you.

If the above description hasn't quite whet your appetite then take heed for there are two very worthwhile things to consider before writing off a photographic jaunt up this modest little hill; the ease of ascent and the enormous view from the top. Moel y Ci presents the mountains' last gasp before plunging down to the coastal plains and as such offers a view of Anglesey in its entirety. It is the views inland though, that really hold the gaze which sweep from the Carneddau foothills in the east right around to Yr Eifl on the Lleyn Peninsula, a monster mountain panorama!

What to shoot and viewpoints

This location is all about grand vistas and a wide angle lens is essential for capturing those sweeping views.

Viewpoint 1 – The lower slopes

From the water works turn right and follow the road for 250 metres before crossing over and going through an old metal kissing gate. A grassy path slants gently up the side of Moel y Ci before meeting another gate and intersecting walls which can be used to great effect as compositional tools. From the walls an obvious path climbs more steeply and the views south expand almost with every step so don't neglect to look behind you!

Viewpoint 2 – The Plateau

After a short ascent you'll find yourself on a broad heathery plateau. It's well worth exploring the whole area if you have time but advantage should definitely be taken of the rock outcrops which act as foreground interest for the sweeping views of the surrounding mountains. A little further on is the trig point and summit shelter where you'll find a perfectly ergonomic arrangement of rocks on which to relax out of the wind!

Opposite: VP 2. The southern panorama from Moel y Ci on a beautiful May evening. Six shot stitched panorama. Canon 7D, 17-40mm at 17mm, ISO 100, 1/8 sec at f/11, tripod, 0.9 graduated filter.

How to get here

From the southern outskirts of Bethesda quit the main A5 trunk road for the B4409 which is signed 'Zip World Snowdonia'. Follow the road for just over a kilometre and turn left at the Bradite Paint factory (also signed for Mynydd Llandegai). The road rises steeply into Mynydd Llandegai trending sharply right before meeting a crossroads at the junction of Llwybr Main and Lon Hermon. Go straight ahead and turn left at the next crossroads. After a third of a mile you will arrive at the water works where, with care and consideration, a car can be left.

Parking postcode: LL57 4EJ
Parking grid ref: SH 59516 65526
Parking lat/long: 53.168278, -4.103271
Map: OS Explorer Map OL17 (1:25 000) Snowdon/Conwy Valley

Accessibility

This is a very easy walk and the distance from car to the summit trig point is a little less than one mile involving 114 metres of ascent. The path is clear throughout, easy to follow and can be done in trainers although there can be boggy sections on the plateau where boots may be appreciated.

Best time of year/day

Sitting at the northern extremity of the Snowdonian highlands and with an unobstructed western horizon Moel y Ci is very much a sunset location and one for all seasons. If there is any light to be had during the evening golden hour it will almost certainly be falling on Moel y Ci.

Top left: VP 1. Looking south along the wall to Parc Drysgol and Moel Eilio in warm October light. Canon 7D, 17-40mm at 20mm, ISO 100, 02.5 sec at f/11, tripod, 0.9 graduated filter.
Top right: VP 2. Asperitas clouds gathering over the Carneddau on a May evening. Canon 7D, 17-40mm at 19mm, ISO 100, 1 sec at f/14, tripod, 0.9 graduated filter.

02 PEN YR OLE WEN

Standing as the cornerstone of the Ogwen and Nant Ffrancon valleys, Pen yr Ole Wen is muscular brute and its south ridge is one of the most gruelling routes to the top of a Welsh mountain. Consolation for the effort involved in an ascent comes in the form of unparalleled views of Tryfan's West Face and the Glyderau cwms. Take heart, one need not climb to the very top to experience the superlative scenery on offer and a reasonably short walk will gain as much height as is needed to bring it all within the reach of your camera.

This 'relatively' roadside location is perfect if you only have an hour or two to spare but want to take full-blooded mountain photographs without the commitment of a longer day. It is also a useful option if you want to take a punt in 'iffy' weather but don't fancy embarking on a major mission.

What to shoot and viewpoints

Viewpoint 1 – The Afon Ogwen

From the Ogwen Cottage visitor centre cross the A5 and follow it leftwards over the bridge (Pont y Benglog) where you'll reach a novel stile which bears an inscription in memory of Alf Embleton, an activist involved in the fight for access to hills and moorland in the 1930s. Across the stile you have the Afon Ogwen on your right and a short, scrambly groove system that leads past a couple of holly trees to the main Pen yr Ole Wen path.

That's all to come, but first there is a bonus location within spitting distance. Descend a short way down easy but polished rocky steps (slippery when wet) to get right beside the infant Afon Ogwen. From here there is a good path which follows the northern shore of Llyn Ogwen but without going too far decent compositions can be found. Late evenings are a good time to shoot here as low light enables a longer shutter speed with which to add a little movement to the water and Tryfan, which dominates the background, is often beautifully illuminated.

Top left: VP 1. The Afon Ogwen with Tryfan and Glyder Fach glowing beyond on an April evening. Four shot stitched panorama. Canon 7D, 17-40mm at 17mm, ISO 100, 3.2sec at f/11, 0.9 graduated filter, tripod.

Top right: VP 2. Tryfan catching the last sliver of late July light. Canon 6D, 24-70 at 24mm, ISO 100, 0.3sec at f/11, 0.9 graduated filter, tripod.

Bottom left: VP 2. Cwm Idwal in September Stormlight. Canon 6D, 24-70mm at 57mm, ISO 100, 1/40 sec at f/8, polarising filter, 0.9 graduated filter, tripod

Bottom right: VP 2. Looking down into Cwm Idwal on a colourful July evening. Canon 6D, 24-70 at 24mm, ISO 100, 1/4sec at f/11, 0.9 graduated filter, tripod.

How to get here

Park at Ogwen Cottage in the Ogwen Valley. Ogwen Cottage lies on the main A5 trunk road and be easily accessed from the east, 10 miles from Betws y Coed; or the north, 4.5 miles from Bethesda.

Parking postcode: LL57 3LZ
Parking grid ref: OS SH 64904 60412
Parking lat/long: 53.123515, -4.019966
Map: OS Explorer Map OL17 (1:25 000) Snowdon / Conwy Valley

Accessibility

The way up to the shoulder on Pen yr Ole Wen follows a good but steep path all the way with a brief easy scramble at the start. In the winter months it is rarely affected by severe conditions but when snow lies at valley level care should be taken and crampons/axe considered essential items.

The rocks beside the Afon Ogwen can be greasy when wet and the riverside can be dangerous in periods of spate.

Best time of year/day

The lie of the land dictates that the best time for the early riser is mid October if foreground light is required and the summer months for light on the mountains. As a sunset location May to late July are best with Winter being the trickiest season to shoot; the south facing aspect means shooting into the sun for most of the day.

Next spread: VP 2. Epic atmosphere building over Y Gribin on a September afternoon. Canon 6D, 24-70 at 70mm, ISO 100, 1/40sec at f/7.1, 0.6 -0.9 graduated filter, circular polarising filter, tripod.

02 PEN YR OLE WEN

Viewpoint 2 – The Shoulder of Pen yr Ole Wen
Time to move on and as you retrace your steps a
curious artefact and point of interest comes into view.
Below Pont y Benglog there is a perfectly preserved
packhorse bridge beneath the main arch. It has been
suggested that it may be of Roman origin but it is most
likely part of an old drover's route.

Back above the river the scrambly grooves (now on
the right) are tackled before a good path climbs steeply
up heathery slopes before arriving at a broad grassy
shoulder 240 metres above the Ogwen Valley. On your
left is a rocky knoll topped with two perched boulders
and that's where the gold is!

An impressive vista lies before you and the temptation
is to try and cram it all in. However, this is a spot where
panoramic images fall short as the compositions tend to
be very unbalanced. The trick here is in utilising the excellent
foreground opportunities and 'working' the scene to create
a strong composition. With that in mind it may appear
at first glance that there are only a couple of shots to
be had but with a little imagination the scope widens.
This comes into play when forgoing the bigger picture
and working with longer focal lengths, especially when
atmospheric or changeable conditions prevail. Focusing
your attention on interesting elements, simplifying the
scene and concentrating on shape and form can lead to
very strong images when light and land come together.

03 CWM IDWAL

"A house burnt down by fire did not tell its story more plainly than did this valley".

These are the words of Charles Darwin, referring to the classic post-glacial landscape of Cwm Idwal after his visit in 1831. Long before Mr Darwin's arrival it is said that the cwm and its llyn were named after Idwal, the handsome and intelligent son of Owain, prince of Gwynedd. The boy was entrusted into the care of Nefydd Hardd whose own son Dunawd was rather dim by comparison, lacking Idwal's obvious talents. Jealousy, or so the story goes, gets the better of Nefydd and Idwal, unable to swim, is pushed into the lake, perishing in its silent depths. In modern times the cwm has become a mecca for geologists, botanists, climbers, walkers and, in increasing numbers, photographers.

Cwm Idwal is a photo-location of the highest quality and a circuit around Llyn Idwal reveals one superb viewpoint after another. To experience such dramatic glacial scenery usually requires a hefty walk in, but much of Idwal's appeal lies in its accessibility. An easy stroll of around 15 minutes will take you from your car into a prime landscape rich in pictorial opportunities in all but the filthiest of weather conditions.

What to shoot and viewpoints

A photographic walk around Cwm Idwal is ostensibly about shooting by the water's edge and most will not stray too far from the lower path that encircles the llyn. From the 'beach' on the llyn's northern shore panoramic images of the cwm are all worth trying especially if the water is still. Elsewhere the upper path gives enough elevation for excellent wide shots of the llyn backed by Pen yr Ole Wen. An alternative approach via either bank of the Afon Idwal will keep you away from the crowds and opens up possibilities for unusual compositions.

Tryfan and the Afon Idwal on a March afternoon. Canon 6D, 24-70mm at 28mm, ISO 100, 1/5 sec at f/22, tripod, polarising filter, 0.9 graduated filter.

How to get here

Ogwen Cottage lies on the main A5 trunk road and is easily accessed from the east (10 miles from Betws y Coed) or the north (four and a half miles from Bethesda).

Parking postcode: LL57 3LZ
Parking grid ref: OS SH 64904 60412
Parking lat/long: 53.123711, -4.0203282
Map: OS Explorer Map OL17 (1:25 000)
Snowdon / Conwy Valley

Accessibility

An engineered path leads into the cwm from behind the visitor centre and continues all the way round the llyn including the upper route via a slab bridge across Idwal stream which until recently acted as a natural 'Granny Stopper'. An approach via the Afon Idwal can be boggy and negotiates boulders which can be greasy when wet.

Best time of year/day

As a target for traditional 'golden hour' light Cwm Idwal struggles in many respects. It's north-facing aspect denies foreground lighting until the sun is high in the sky for most of the year. The best conditions, in my opinion, come on days of gloomy or changeable weather when dark, foreboding scenes can, with a little imagination, be captured from dawn 'till dusk. Under snow the cwm is also a relatively safe place for less experienced walkers to photograph epic mountain scenery without the commitment required of higher and more remote locations.

*Opposite top left: Y Garn across a frozen Llyn Idwal on a February morning. Canon 7D, 17-24mm at 17mm, ISO 100, 1/200 sec at f/8, tripod, 0.6 graduated filter. **Top right**: Llyn Idwal and Pen yr Ole Wen on a bleak January afternoon. Canon 6D, 24-70mm at 29mm, ISO 100, 0.3 sec at f/8, tripod, polarising filter, 0.9 graduated filter.*

Opposite: Idwal reflections on a November morning. Canon 6D, 24-70mm at 31mm, ISO 100, 2.5 sec at f/22, tripod, polarising filter, 0.9 graduated filter.

04 LLYNNAU MYMBYR

Any photography guide to Snowdonia would be incomplete without including Llynnau Mymbyr, Capel Curig's twin lakes and home to arguably the finest roadside view in Wales. There are many photo-locations in Britain which have achieved classic status, all of them are well known and have been extensively shot. They're 'classic' for a very good reason, and that is because they're accessible and extremely beautiful. With virtually no effort required – other than a one minute walk – this iconic viewpoint can be visited repeatedly until you get the shot you're after and even then, you will want to return as no two days here are ever quite the same. Llynnau Mymbyr represents the ultimate in instant photographic gratification, a guilty pleasure which, on occasion, even I can't resist!

There are several spots in the vicinity of the llyn which are worth exploring but the most sought after and the one featured here is the easiest to attain and, as it happens, the best of the bunch. It can be no coincidence, then, that in 1801 the Capel Curig Inn (later the Royal Hotel) was built at the foot of the lake to take advantage of this peerless scene. In 1955 the Royal Hotel was renamed Plas y Brenin and to this day remains as the 'National Mountain Sports Centre'.

What to shoot and viewpoints

From the lay-by walk towards Plas y Brenin and go through the gate on the right. A stepped path leads down to the lake and footbridge. At the lakeside water levels can vary greatly depending on rainfall so your favourite boulder may be submerged which will force you to really look around and find new compositions.

Opposite: Snowdon bathed in October dawn light. Canon 6D, 24-70mm at 44mm, ISO 100, 30 sec at f/11, tripod, 6 stop ND filter, 0.6 graduated filter.

A September morning beside Llynnau Mymbyr. Canon 6D, 24-70mm at 55mm, ISO 100, 1/25 sec at f/8, tripod, polarising filter.

How to get here

The parking area is immediately west of Plas y Brenin on the A4086 which lies a short distance beyond the junction of the A5 at Capel Curig.

Parking postcode: LL24 0ET
Parking grid ref: SH 715578
Parking lat/long: 53.102269, -3.918910
Map: OS Explorer Map OL17 (1:25 000)
Snowdon / Conwy Valley

Accessibility

This is the most accessible location in the book and as such is good bet for a last dash shoot if time is against you. The grassy lake shore is rough and tussocky with many ruts and holes which offer great opportunities for breaking an ankle. The boulders at the water's edge are very slippery when wet so all in all a measured approach to shooting is recommended.

Best time of year/day

My preference is for dawn shoots in autumn and winter but colourful sunsets can erupt at any time of the year. The lake is often still when others are not and perfectly reflect the classic outline of the Snowdon Horseshoe. In winter it is not unusual for the lake to freeze as it is relatively shallow.

Above: A stunning November sunset.
Canon 7D, 17-40mm at 17mm, ISO 100, 13 sec at f/11, tripod, 0.9 graduated filter.

Above: First light on a chilly morning in March.
Canon 7D, 17-40mm at 23mm, ISO 100, 1/10 sec at f/11, tripod, 0.6 graduated filter.

05 MOEL BERFEDD AND CWMFFYNNON

As the A4086 climbs up to Pen y Pass it traverses the slopes of a nondescript rock-girt hump at which most won't bat an eyelid. That hump is Moel Berfedd. On its pathless summit there lies a tale of neglect while half a kilometre away a large car park buzzes with activity and blazed trails wind their way into the Snowdon Massif. A hill with very few suitors it may be, but lowly Moel Berfedd is all the better for it and is a revelation when upon its craggy top you stand for the first time and look across to peaks which rise to over twice its height. To photograph such an impressive view usually means investing in some serious physical effort but this location is relatively easy to reach and is perfect for sunrise shoots.

Complementing the rewarding vista from up high there are watery delights to be had below in the form of Llyn Cwmffynnon which occupies a large secluded cwm beneath the high tops of the Glyderau. A good half day can be spent exploring the environs of Moel Berfedd and Cwmffynnon where the illusion of wilderness is accompanied by a solitude you would only expect to find in a more remote area.

What to shoot and viewpoints

Moel Berfedd stands at the head of three valleys and commands exceptional views down all of them. Big, chest beating mountain images are the order of the day with the Snowdon range taking centre stage and looking absolutely magnificent. Lakeside shots work very well from its northern end and a thorough examination of the outflow stream can be an especially profitable exercise.

Viewpoint 1 – Moel Berfedd

From the car park cross the road and go through a gate/stile on the left-hand side of the youth hostel. A path leads up and left until it the ground flattens out. Turn right and follow a faint path up through rock outcrops from the top of which the A4086 can be seen snaking through the valley into the distance. The road provides a wonderful leading line with Crib Goch towering above. By excluding the road and using some of the excellent foregrounds hereabouts it is possible to take photographs with an altogether wilder feel. Llyn Cwmffynnon has also revealed itself and this is a good place to capture its foreboding black waters. From the outcrops drop down into a boggy depression and cross a stile. From here Moel Berfedd is obvious and a brief climb up grassy couloirs will land you on the summit where the view suddenly expands to include the lonely valley of Dyffryn Mymbyr and the lush pastures of Nant Gwynant.

Pen y Pass is on the A4086, 5 miles from Capel Curig and 5 miles from Llanberis. From Capel Curig leave the A5 at the junction of the A4086 (Pinnacle Pursuits general store on the corner) and follow the road before turning right just after the Pen y Gwryd Hotel. From Llanberis simply drive up the A4086 to Pen y Pass.

Parking postcode: LL55 4NY
Parking grid ref: SH 64737 55628
Parking lat/long: 53.080942, -4.021212
Map: OS Explorer Map OL17 (1:25 000) Snowdon / Conwy Valley

Accessibility

This is an easy mountain photography walk of 1.8 miles / 3km with 160 metres of ascent for a round trip including the circumnavigation of Llyn Cwmffynnon. Objective hazards are few even under snow condition but the whole area can be very marshy and vigilance is required to avoid the deeper bogs. Gaiters are a very good idea if you wish to remain dry shod. If in spate do not attempt to cross the Nant Gwryd stream as the rocks become very greasy when wet and the water is fast flowing.

Best time of year/day

A wall of high mountains block out the western horizon so seekers of golden hour light will have make use of dawn for which Moel Berfedd excels year-round. In autumn the grasses of hill and cwm turn a very attractive straw colour which catches the light beautifully and contrasts well with the heather of the Glyderau slopes. These are very worthy locations to take a chance on during changeable days of sunshine and showers where dramatic storm light can repay the meagre effort of a visit in spades.

Top left: *VP 1. A November dawn on Moel Berfedd.*
Canon 7D, 17-40mm at 17mm, ISO 100, 1/60
sec at f/11, tripod, 0.6 - 0.9 graduated filters.

Above: *VP 1. The view down into Nant Gwynant*
from Moel Berfedd on a February afternoon.
Canon 7D, 17-40mm at 17mm, ISO 100, 1/160
sec at f/11, tripod, 0.6–0.9 graduated filters.

VP 1. Looking down a frosty Mymbyr valley
towards Capel Curig on a March morning.
Canon 7D, 17-40mm at 17mm, ISO 100,
1/20 sec at f/11,tripod, 0.9 graduated filter.

Overleaf: *VP 1. Crib Goch and the Pass of*
Llanberis on an October afternoon.
Canon 6D, 24 - 70mm at 24mm, ISO 100,
1/100 sec at f/8, 0.9 graduated filter, tripod.

VP 1. Crib Goch and the Pass of Llanberis on an October afternoon. Canon 6D, 24-70mm at 24mm, ISO 100, 1/100 sec at f/8, 0.9 graduated filter, tripod.

VP 1. Crib Goch from below Moel Berfedd on an October morning. Canon 6D, 24-70mm at 27mm, ISO 100, 1/30 sec at f/16, 0.9 graduated filter, tripod.

VP 1. Llyn Cwmffynnon and the high tops of the Glyderau on a stormy October morning. Canon 6D, 24-70mm at 26mm, ISO 100, 1/80 sec at f/8, 0.9 graduated filter.

VP 2. Autumn colours beside the Nant Gwryd stream on an October afternoon. Canon 6D, 24-70mm at 30mm, ISO 100, 1/5 sec at f/16, polarising filter, 0.9 graduated filter, tripod.

**Viewpoint 2 – Llyn Cwmffynnon and
the Nant Gwryd stream**

The descent from Moel Berfedd is a 'go where you please' affair heading generally northwards but trending left as height is lost. The ground by the lake is often very wet but by heading for its east shore a path can be picked up which eventually leads to a stile crossing. If the lake is still (a rare occurrence) then advantage should be taken of its reflective qualities before following the infant Afon Nant Gwryd downstream to where a series of small cascades offer up some good compositions with the river leading the eye into a scene backed by Crib Goch's pyramidal form. This is a wonderful place to take photographs and you will feel totally cut off from civilisation with neither a road or building in sight. By retracing your steps back towards the stile you can cross the stream and continue your journey with a circumnavigation of the lake where you will come upon small pools which throw up interesting compositional opportunities. However, after rain it may not be possible to find a safe point to cross, in which case a return by the way you came is the most sensible option.

*VP 1. The Snowdon Massif catching first light on a
March morning. 6 shot stitched panorama.
Canon 7D, 17-40mm at 17mm, ISO 100, 1/5 sec
at f/11, tripod, 0.6 graduated filter.*

06 LLANBERIS AND 'THE PASS'

The bustling little village of Llanberis gives its name to the famous road pass which makes its way through some of the most arresting mountain scenery in Britain and rises to 1178 feet above sea level at Gorphwysfa. Each year at Gorphwysfa – more commonly known as Pen y Pass – hundreds of thousands of people begin their walk to Yr Wyddfa (Snowdon), the highest peak south of the border. It's the same deal back in Llanberis although the numbers are augmented by 130,000 others who annually make the pilgrimage via the Snowdon Mountain Railway. In between these two very different places you will find enough photographic inspiration to keep you busy on occasions when the heights are shrouded in mist or a more sedate outing is called for.

Although barely scratching the surface of what would be possible during a prolonged exploration a diverse range of subject matter is hinted at including waterfalls, lakes, people watching and classic landscape scenes. All the locations in this chapter have their own parking spots and can be visited individually or picked off one after another on a grand tour of Llanberis and the pass.

What to shoot and viewpoints

Viewpoint 1 – Pen y Pass

All manner of human life congregates at this large car park which services the needs of Snowdon walkers and guests at the adjacent youth hostel, a place of great historical significance in the story of British mountaineering. More often than not the area is teeming with people but a short walk west of the car park will find you alone with your thoughts and a grandstand view of the pass. This is a great place to use the road as a lead line into the narrow jaws of the valley and your next location.

Viewpoint 2 – The Cromlech Boulders

The Cromlech boulders are huge lumps of rock which have fallen from great heights to rest on the valley floor. They are extremely popular with 'boulderers', a sub-species of climber endowed with super-human strength and swollen forearms. While not intrinsically interesting in themselves, the area around the boulders certainly is. Several lay-bys allow convenient parking spots from which to survey an impressive array of crags upon which deeds of daring do are played out in full view of incredulous and voyeuristic motorists. Summer evenings are a prime time for this unique form of people watching and a long lens is useful for 'pulling in' the action with the climbers adding a real sense of scale to an alarmingly vertical landscape. On the southern side of the road riverside shots are possible and a host of gnarled hawthorns also provide many photographic possibilities.

How to get here

All the locations are on or close by the A4086 which runs between Llanberis and Capel Curig.

Parking grid ref: Pen y Pass – SH 64737 55589;
Cromlech Boulders – SH 62830 56683;
Nant Peris – SH 59818 58728;
Dolbadarn Castle – SH 58677 59678;
The Lonely Tree – SH 57335 60916;
Pen Llyn – SH 55948 62300

Map: OS Explorer Map OL17 (1:25 000) Snowdon / Conwy Valley

Accessibility

The majority of these locations are genuinely roadside (with the exception of Nant Peris) meaning that persons of limited mobility can access and enjoy their photography.

Best time of year/day

Interesting images can be made at all the locations year-round, in most weather conditions and from dawn to dusk.

Opposite left: VP 2. An old Hawthorn at the end of a June day. Canon 7D, 17-40mm at 17mm, ISO 100, 1/25 sec at f/8.

Opposite right: VP 2. Climbers on 'Hangover' E1 5b on Clogwyn y Grochan – May evening. Canon 6D, 70-300mm at 300mm, ISO 1600, 1/400 sec at f/8.

VP2. Dinas Cromlech briefly revealed on a filthy September day. Canon 6D, 24-70mm at 70mm, ISO 100, 1/80 sec at f/6.3.

VP2. Dinas Cromlech catching late light on a September evening. Canon 6D, 24-70mm at 45mm, ISO 100, 1/125 sec at f/6.3, 0.9 graduated filter, tripod.

Viewpoint 3 – Nant Peris and Dolbadarn Castle

The lay-by beneath 'Ben's Bunkhouse' (at the south-eastern end of Llyn Peris) is your next port of call. Cross the road and turn right for 150 metres where a gate gives access (via a track) to a network of footpaths which criss-cross small rocky hillocks. There is much scope here for original compositions in a place where few others bother to roam. The view up the pass is sublime and in early spring bluebells are abundant. Back at the lay-by a short drive (or wander) of a mile will take you to the remains of Dolbadarn Castle, a 13 century fortification built by Llywelyn the Great and a wonderful place in which to make a photographic connection between Welsh history, culture and the landscape which ties it all together. It can be a busy spot which makes 'clean' shots a tricky proposition. This location quietens down in the evenings which, incidentally, is when the best light occurs.

Viewpoint 4 – Ceunant Mawr

Tucked away and hidden from all but those travelling on the Snowdon Railway is Llanberis' very own waterfall, Ceunant Mawr. Free parking for the waterfall can be problematic in that it is in a residential area with limited provision for visitor's vehicles. From Dolbadarn, however, it is less than a one kilometre walk to the falls. Turn right, follow the road to the Victoria Hotel and turn left at the mini roundabout onto Victoria Terrace. After 250 metres turn right and follow the road beneath the railway bridge. As the road bares left a signed track climbs up to the upper viewing area, to which access is gained by

(carefully) crossing the Snowdon Railway. The view from here is good but obstructed by the branches of surrounding trees. A better bet is to seek out the lower part of the falls which is reached by ignoring the signed track and taking a muddy path to the left which passes underneath the bridge. Depending on the volume of water there are many compositions available with autumn being the best time for a visit.

Viewpoint 5 – The Lonley Tree of Llyn Padarn

This iconic birch requires little in the way of introduction and has become something of a cliché in recent years. That said, no photographic guide to Llanberis would be complete without a mention of the 'Lonely Tree' and there can be few folk who are able resist this guilty pleasure when visiting the area. The main attraction of this location is the subject matter itself which can be shot morning, noon and night in most conditions year-round. The ideal is calm waters, good light and interesting skies but if the lake is choppy and the light flat then long exposures can save the day. To find the Lonely Tree is relatively simple. Around 300 metres past the main Llyn Padarn car park (look for a big rusty sword!) turn right and then right again into a large parking area. From top left hand side (north west) of the car park a path through the trees will lead you in about 30 seconds to the unmistakeable, much loved and much photographed location.

Viewpoint 6 – Pen Llyn

A classic lakeside view which is as accessible as they come and speaks for itself. Here at the head of Llyn Padarn the Welsh highlands abruptly give way to the coastal lowlands. Sunrise and sunsets are the order of the day with wide and telephoto shots working equally well. As with the 'lonely tree' still days offer the most pleasing results. To get there drive out of Llanberis and turn right onto the A4244 (signed Bangor) and right again after 180 metres. The bridge and viewpoint are on your left and parking on your right.

Top left: VP 3. A cloud-capped Snowdon from Dinas high above Nant Peris on a June evening. Canon 7D, 17-40mm at 17mm, ISO 100, 1/25 sec at f/8, 0.6 graduated filter, tripod.

Top right: VP 5. The famous 'lonely tree' of Llyn. Padarn on an August evening. Canon 7D, 17-40mm at 17mm, ISO 100, 0.6 sec at f/11, 0.6 graduated filter, tripod.

Opposite: VP 6. A beautiful September evening at Pen Llyn. Canon 6D, 24-70mm at 24mm, ISO 100, 0.6 sec at f/11, 0.9 graduated filter, tripod.

07 LLYN Y DYWARCHEN AND CLOGWYN Y GARREG

At the summit of the Drws y Coed Pass little Llyn y Dywarchen – lake of the turf island or floating sod as some would have it – nestles in a hollow between the steep sides of Y Garn and Mynydd Mawr. Unseen by those travelling through the pass it is a refuge of the Tylwyth Teg, a race of mischievous Welsh fairies which, though often grotesque in appearance, have the power to seduce and capture men who blunder unsuspectingly into their domain. Gentlemen, you have been warned. The synonymous 'turf island' has long since disappeared but was documented by many credible witnesses who visited the lake from twelfth century historian Geraldus Cambrensis to the celebrated comet botherer Edmond Halley.

The circumnavigation of this enchanted body of water – which also serves as an ideal location for a quick evening photography hit – is a delightful outing which offers enough variety to fill a morning or afternoon. As a bonus there is Clogwyn y Garreg, a fine pint-sized peak that apes its bigger brother Mynydd Mawr.

What to shoot and viewpoints

Viewpoint 1 – Llyn y Dywarchen

An anti-clockwise walk around the llyn is the logical approach and the first obvious subject is the boathouse which acts to 'anchor' long exposures, along with two boats in situ beside the small concrete jetty. By mounting the hummock directly behind the boat house an island comes into view which resembles a surfacing whale. This feature becomes very colourful in autumn. Next, at the south east corner of the llyn a series of boggy pools form effective foregrounds and often catch the reflection of Mynydd Mawr. One of the finest compositions can be found at the llyn's north western corner where a tree, old ruin and fence combine to produce pleasing images.

Viewpoint 2 – Clogwyn y Garreg

The vast majority of images you will see of Llyn y Dywarchen are taken from the water's edge with most photographers completely ignoring the possibilities offered from the peak rising above the llyn's northern shore. Quite why this is so is a mystery as on my first visit many years ago I made a beeline for it, getting involved in some hair-raising scrambling in the process. Fear not, there is a very easy way to the summit which is gained by a five minute plod up the blunt ridge to the right of the craggy face. At the top you will find a super view down the Nantlle and Colwyn valleys along with an aerial view of Llyn y Dywarchen and Llyn y Gader. Foregrounds are tricky here but with perseverance can be made to work or eliminated for simpler compositions. Descend the way you came and don't be tempted to force a direct way down.

How to get here

There is room for half a dozen cars directly beneath the dam which is found close to Rhyd Ddu village on the B4418. Western approaches are made via Penygroes and Nantlle.

Parking postcode: LL54 6TP
Parking grid ref: SH558 533
Parking lat/long: 53.053452, -4.136550
Map: OS Explorer Map OL17 (1:25 000) Snowdon / Conwy Valley

Accessibility

While walking around the lake involves no appreciable height gain the ground can make for difficult going on tussocks and through bogs. The use of gaters, if not essential, should be considered if one is to remain dry shod. The ascent of Clogwyn y Garreg is brief and not difficult but the utmost care should be taken when exploring its Southern edge which is precipitous and extremely unforgiving.

Best time of year/day

The llyn is good for year round landscape photography with autumn, winter and spring being the most favourable seasons. On Clogwyn y Garreg the two weeks either side of the spring and autumn equinoxes are by far the best times to visit for striking side-lit conditions.

Top: Looking towards a cloud-capped Snowdon on a March evening. Six shot stitched panorama. Canon 7D, 17-40mm at 20mm, ISO 100, 1 sec at f/16, tripod, 0.9 graduated filter.

Bottom: Llyn y Dywarchen from Clogwyn y Garreg on a March evening. Six shot stitched panorama. Canon 7D, 17-40mm at 17mm, ISO 100, 0.6 sec at f/11, tripod. 0.6 graduated filter.

08 NANT GWYNANT AND LLYN GWYNANT

Of all the valleys in Northern Snowdonia, Nant Gwynant is perhaps the most picturesque. In stark contrast to the austere environs of Dyffryn Mymbyr which, in all probability, you will have passed through to get there, the scene is one of extravagant beauty which even the most jaded photographer will find irresistible. A romantic lake, pockets of ancient woodland and the surrounding hills coalesce to form an extremely photogenic whole.

You could wander around Nant Gwynant for weeks before getting to know the valley's many nooks and crannies but the three locations featured here are a good starting point for further exploration. The two roadside viewpoints are well known to photographers such is their ease of access while the Bwlch Rhediad path, which requires a little more effort, is known only to a few and gives an unusual perspective on a much photographed valley.

What to shoot and viewpoints

Viewpoint 1 – Hafod Rhisgl Farm and Nant Gwynant

The main Snowdon viewpoint on the A498 is very popular with tourists and although it presents an impressive view of the mountain it is marred by the unsightly Cwm Dyli pipeline and fails to disclose the full length of Llyn Gwynant.

A more pleasing vista can be found from the first lay-by as you travel towards the lake at SH 65777 52988.

A gate leads onto a promontory of scrubby grass above Hafod Rhisgl farm and looks straight down the barrel of Nant Gwynant. It's tempting to just 'spray and pray' here but careful composition makes all the difference between a snap and a great photographic image. Fill the frame with interest and exclude distracting elements.

This particular location is great on days of changeable conditions when showers are blown through on the wind and the valley is struck by shafts of light. It's great fun to sit in the car and watch the weather before dashing out on a mission when a window of opportunity arises.

Viewpoint 2 – The path to Bwlch Rhediad

A little further down the road at SH 65699 52698 is another lay-by which gives access to a seldom seen view. Cross the road, go through the gate and follow a path (ignoring the bridleway on the right) which snakes up into broad leafed woodland before emerging onto a bracken-clad hill side. This is the path to Bwlch Rhediad, a very old route which links Gwynant and the Lledr Valley.

There are a few useful devices to aid composition including old walls and gnarled hawthorns but cleaner, less cluttered arrangements can be had by gaining one of the rocky knolls and shooting Llyn Gwynant, the star of the show, in the context of its mountainous setting.

How to get here

The A498 runs through Nant Gwynant from the Pen y Gwryd/Llanberis junction down to Beddgelert. Llyn Gwynant is 6.8 miles from Capel Curig and 3.7 miles from Beddgelert.

Parking postcode: LL55 4NP
Parking grid ref: SH 64907 51972
Parking lat/long: 53.047892, -4.0167344
Map: OS Explorer Map OL17 (1:25 000) Snowdon/Conwy Valley

Accessibility

Viewpoints one and three are literally a few metres from the lay-bys while viewpoint two requires an uphill walk of 0.5km with 160 metres of ascent taking around half an hour.

Best time of year/day

Strong images from all three locations can be made year-round and in autumn the valley is especially beautiful when the abundant woodland takes on seasonal colour and morning mists are a common occurrence. Due to Nant Gwynant's north east-south west alignment sunsets are better in the winter months and while the same is generally true for sunrise shoots early light can be very good throughout the year.

Top left: VP 1. Hafody Rhisgl farm on a stormy May afternoon. Canon 7D, 17-40mm at 26mm, ISO 100, 1/50sec at f/8, 0.9 graduated filter.

Top right: VP 2. An autumn pre-dawn high above Nant Gwynant – late September. Canon 6D, 24-70mm at 24mm, ISO 100, 3.2sec at f/11, 0.9 graduated filter, tripod.

Opposite: VP 3. Morning mist-March. Canon 7D, 17-40mm at 17mm, ISO 100, 1/15sec at f/11, tripod.

Viewpoint 3 – Llyn Gwynant Lakeshore

The southern shore of the lake has a number of small lay-bys from which to examine the various bays, each of which offer subtly different views and compositional opportunities. It is possible to walk most of the way around Llyn Gwynant off road on decent paths so with time to spare a pleasant hour can be spent recceing locations for future reference.

Staying roadside, the biggest factor in how your images will pan out is the time of day and prevailing lighting conditions which can transform the atmosphere in an instant. As with many lakeside scenes reflections can really put the icing on the cake so if you arrive and the lake is still you must be quick as you won't have long to set up before a seagull or duck – hell bent on stealing your sandwiches – happens by to break the mirror.

VP 3. Yr Aran reflected in the still waters of a January morning. Canon 7D, 17-40mm at 40mm, ISO 100, 1/13 sec at f/11, tripod.

VP 3. First light on Yr Aran on a frosty November morning. Canon 6D, 24-70mm at 30mm, ISO 100, 4 sec at f/11, circular polarising filter, 0.9 graduated filter, tripod.

09 CARREG HYLLDREM

Unless you are a very capable rock climber you will probably not have heard of Carreg Hylldrem, and even then it is unlikely. As an impending bastion towering above the A4085 Aberglaslyn to Penrhyndeudraeth road it is palpably out of bounds for the average photographer but looks can be deceiving. Although the crag is clearly unassailable to mere mortals it forms the end of long ridge which is easily accessed in less than 15 minutes from the road.

This is one of those closely guarded 'secret' locations known to few ... until now that is! A place where bootprints and tripod holes are absent Carreg Hylldrem is a roadside location par excellence where well-loved mountains are seen in a new and exciting light.

What to shoot and viewpoints

The ridge runs SW to NE and being on the edge of the once sandy expanse of Traeth Mawr gives unbroken coastal views. However, like Moel y Ci, the main interest for mountain photographers is the inland panorama which forms a great arc of shapely peaks from Moel Ddu to Cnicht and the Moelwynion with the regal Snowdon Massif taking centre stage.

The ridge top is grassy but furnished with outcropping rock, an ideal place then to practise 'working a location', playing with the elements of the scene and solving the little puzzles that are thrown up by the many foreground possibilities.

To gain this revealing podium leave the car and walk towards the bridge (Pont Garreg Hylldrem) taking the track to its left signed for Gelli. After about 20 metres climb steeply into the woods, trending leftwards towards the crag where a faint path develops over mossy boulders. A bracken-choked saddle is soon underfoot and all that remains is to turn right for a short climb onto the ridge where a spectacular vista greets you.

How to get here

On the A4085 at the foot of Carreg Hylldrem and beside the Afon Croesor is a small lay-by with room for two or three cars. From Beddgelert take the A498 through the Aberglaslyn Gorge heading for Porthmadog until a left turn over the bridge (Pont Aberglaslyn) and onto the A4085 (approximately 4.3 miles). The A4085 can also be accessed from Penrhyndeudraeth (if travelling from Porthmadog, Harlech or Blaenau Ffestiniog) with parking just under 3 miles from the village high street.

Parking postcode: LL48 6SH
Parking grid ref: SH 61518 43116
Parking lat/long: 52.967528, -4.063462
Map: OS Explorer Map OL18 (1:25 000) Harlech, Porthmadog & Bala/Y Bala

Accessibility

Although the walk up to the ridge is very short it is steep and a mixture of leaf litter and boulders can make it very slippery so a good pair of boots are recommended. During late spring and summer tall, dense bracken conceals the path at the saddle so care should be taken with foot placements until the ridge is attained.

Best time of year/day

Sitting on the western edge of the National Park and apart from the high mountains means Carreg Hylldrem is a prime spot for golden hour at the end of the day. In this respect November to March is the very best period as the sun sets into the sea without the intervening hills throwing the foreground into shadow. Visiting during changeable weather can also be very profitable year-round and at any time of day when rainbows, racing cloud shadows and slivers of light can make for dramatic images.

Top: Stormy afternoon light from Carreg Hylldrem – September afternoon. Canon 6D, 24-70mm at 24mm, ISO 100, 1/8 sec at f/11, 0.6 graduated filter, tripod.

Bottom: The Snowdon Massif from across Nantmor in vivid evening light – March. Canon 7D, 17-40mm at 40mm, ISO 100, 1/20 sec at f/14, 0.9 graduated filter, tripod.

10 LLYNNAU CREGENNAN AND PARED Y CEFN HIR

Few things are more relaxing for the landscape photographer than to while away several hours at a peaceful lakeside. Time slows down and worldly worries drift away as you quietly make your way from place to place seeking out the best viewpoints. Conversely, the thrill of shooting panoramic images on the crest of a high ridge is hard to beat when the wind is fresh and the vista sublime. If your heart desires the best of both worlds then a trip to this location should top your list of priorities as there is no finer place in the national park at which to enjoy this intoxicating combination.

Llynnau Cregennan are two attractive lakes which sit at 800ft above the Mawddach estuary surrounded by a magnificent mountain backdrop. To the south rises the great escarpment of Cadair Idris while northwards the micro mountain of Pared y Cefn Hir provides a shapely counterpoint to the tranquility of the water's edge. The scenery is both rugged and pastoral with a romantic charm that will make a poet of even the most inarticulate philistine. Should this all sound like hyperbole then there is no reason whatsoever to take my word for it, for the truth, as they say, is out there.

What to shoot and viewpoints

Viewpoint 1 – Lakeside
The larger of the two lakes is the most photographically interesting with its boathouse and wooded island. It is also on Access Land apart from a portion of its southern shore line. That leaves plenty of scope for wandering around and there is a good path which can be used to access the eastern end of Pared y Cefn Hir. Exposed to westerly winds the lakes are rarely still so the use of 6 or 10 stop ND filters can work wonders in smoothing out the surface of the water.

Viewpoint 2 – Pared y Cefn Hir
Old hill forts are scattered all over Snowdonia and their strategic positioning almost always provides spectacular panoramic views; Pared y Cefn Hir is no exception. From the car park turn left and in a short distance go through a gate and follow the left fork of the path as it ascends the hill. There is a short passage of easy scrambling near the top where care should be taken if the rock is wet. The hill itself takes the form of a kilometre long undulating ridge which should be thoroughly explored in order to determine the best vantage points for your compositions. The three main subjects of interest are as follows: the aerial view of Llynnau Cregennan backed by Cadair's western peaks, the seaward vista over the Mawddach Estuary and Cadair Idris itself.

How to get here
Cregennan is 5 miles from Dolgellau and 1.5 miles east of Arthog on the Mawddach section of the A493. From Dolgellau take the Cadair Idris mountain road and follow it for 5 miles until reaching the parking area? Just west of Arthog a steep road rises to the lakes in 1.5 miles. Both roads are single track and gated on the final approach to the lakes. Leave the gates as you find them (usually closed).

Parking postcode: SH 657 143
Parking grid ref: LL39 1LJ
Parking lat/long: 52.708875, -3.987140
Map: OS Explorer Map OL23 (1:25 000) Cadair Idris and Llyn Tegid

Accessibility
In every respect this location is very accessible and the ascent of Pared y Cefn Hir can be made in around twenty minutes. The ground is rough, rocky and heathery on the hill while the lakeside is typically damp in places. Snow on the ground is rare but not unheard of.

Best time of year/day
As with all mountain areas stormy conditions of fast moving clouds will gift the photographer dramatic images through all four seasons and at all times of day. Late light and sunsets are the real forte of this location especially in spring, summer and autumn. Cregennan's wooded island exhibits lovely autumnal colours. It is worth noting that Llynnau Cregennan makes a perfect evening destination after a day on Cadair Idris.

Opposite left: *April evening afterglow over Llynnau Cregennan. Six shot stitched panorama. Canon 7D, 17-40mm at 17mm, ISO 200, 0.3 sec at f/11, tripod, 0.9 graduated filter.*

Opposite right: *An April evening looking over to Barmouth Across the Mawddach Estuary. Canon 7D, 17-40mm at 17mm, ISO 100, 1/5 sec at f/11, tripod, 0.6 and 0.9 graduated filters.*

Above: Looking across Cregennan to Pared y Cefn Hir on a January afternoon. Canon 6D, 24-70mm at 24mm, ISO 100, 30 sec at f/16, tripod, polarising filter, 6 stop ND filter, 0.9 graduated filter.

Above: Late light over Llynnau Cregennan – April. Six shot stitched panorama. Canon 7D, 17-40mm at 17mm, ISO 100, 1/4 sec at f/11, tripod, 0.9 graduated filter.

Companions

Solitude is something that I have come to value over the years and as a necessity for my spiritual well-being it's no surprise that walking alone in the mountains is an important part of my life. At times, however, I enjoy the company of friends who join me for a 'walk' on which I usually harbour the ulterior motive of having them pose for me on some windswept ridge or other, a ruse I often reveal when it's too late for them to say no.

Having companions beside me has enriched so many of my mountain days. The camaraderie, memory making and shared experiences have forged friendships that will last a lifetime. They're an eclectic bunch, my friends, but what we all have in common is an inexhaustible passion for the mountains of Snowdonia. People need people sometimes so, I present to you, the 'usual suspects'.

David Dear

Jed ... and Becca Roberts

David Dear

When I take a shot of Dave and his white hair flashes on my screen I know I'm over-exposed but apart from being an excellent subject from which to take a meter reading Dave has shared more time on the hill with me (and in the pub) than anyone else I know. As a fellow photographer he doesn't mind if I want to stop and take a few minutes to capture an image. More often than not I'm usually waiting for him. We also share a penchant for obscure hills and seeking out corners of Snowdonia where few bother to tread while having a good old blether about politics, music, mountains and Dave's next camera.

Jed ... and Becca Roberts

Jed, with his unique personality and wide vocabulary, was a voracious hill walker and is much missed. He'd usually bring Becca with him and together we'd head into the hills and calm her nerves on exposed ridges or rock steps. The three of us enjoyed many wonderful days in the mountains and Jed's first outing was on Cnicht where he whimpered and wailed in a horizontal hailstorm. Our favourite walk was the round of Marchlyn Mawr and it was always a thrill to look down from Carnedd y Filiast on Becca's childhood home in the Nant Ffrancon. Without fail we would call her parents and waive to them from the top as they watched us through binoculars. 'Holly' joins us on walks now but Jed will never be forgotten.

Dan Lane

Helen Iles

Cat Evans

Jamie Rooke

Dan Lane

Enfant terrible of the Snowdonia landscape photography community, qualified mountain leader and merciless micky taker, Dan has been a close friend since 2013 when I suddenly arrived in North Wales looking for work and somewhere to live. At half my age he is as fit as a fiddle, something which he likes to remind me of when I find myself chasing him up an interminable hillside in search of mountain light. I take consolation in the fact that I take better photographs although it is likely that Dan might have something to say about that, after all, he has an opinion on most things and no doubt he'll put me straight when he reads these words.

Helen Iles

Is there anything this woman can't do? As an ace landscape photographer, member of Barmouth RNLI and the South Snowdonia Mountain Rescue Team, Helen runs the risk of being a bit too awesome for my liking. The fact that she is also a lovely person makes it impossible not to warm to her. Whether in the pub or on the hill she's wonderful company and together we've shared some memorable adventures, most notably our six day mountain leader training course and the gruelling 'Oggie 8' challenge which saw us tackle eight 3000ft mountains to raise funds for the Ogwen Valley Mountain Rescue Team. **www.heleniles.co.uk**

Cat Evans

Having lived her entire life high in the Gwydyr Forest, the stunning panorama of Northern Snowdonia has formed the backdrop to Cat's everyday existence for as long as she can remember. It wasn't until her late teens though that Cat began to hear the call of that distant skyline and feel the need to put those mountains beneath her boots, something I was happy to help with as we worked our way through a list of classic scrambles and hillwalks. Our friendship, however, almost never got started; when our paths first crossed, Cat, in her capacity as a barmaid in our local, had to throw me out of the pub for smoking in the bar! I returned, shamefaced, a few days later and we've been great friends ever since.

Jamie Rooke

Our Jamie is a rough diamond with a glint in his eye, a foul mouth and a swaggering gait which belies a deeper, more thoughtful inner self. Many would say that we exhibit a similar public persona. Our days out are exhausting but stimulating affairs characterised by protracted discourses on philosophy, existential angst and stoicism where, more often than not, we are found to be in violent agreement. Jamie is a qualified Mountain Leader with a special interest in teaching hill skills and empowering others to gain independence in the mountains. **www.exploringsnowdonia.co.uk**

My story, my mountains

"Why do you take photographs, what is your motivation?" Depending on who you ask there are many different answers to this question but mine has always been the same. Put simply, spending time in the great outdoors transformed my life and at the heart of my photography is the desire to communicate that passion and encourage others to seek out the unique gifts that the mountains bestow on us. If you were to take my camera away from me I would still be as eager as ever to get out in the hills but if you took me away from the mountains would I still be so active as a landscape photographer? The answer to that is probably not.

My earliest recollections are of wrecking balls and scenes of decimation during the slum clearances of the early 1970s in Trafford Park, Manchester where my life began. A couple of years later my family moved to the flatlands of East Anglia where I spent the rest of my childhood and remained until my mid-30s. It may seem strange, then, that I came to live a life with the mountains at its very centre. The seeds, however, were sown a long time ago.

My fascination with wild places began as a boy on frequent trips back to Manchester with my grandparents. Our route would always take us through the Peak District where my imagination was gripped by huge 'mountains' and deep valleys drowned by picturesque lakes. Sometimes on Snake Pass the surrounding moors would be cloaked in low-hanging mist and I would simultaneously experience a frisson of terror wondering what might be up there and an inexplicable desire to go and find out for myself. When the distractions of my teenage years arrived, all thoughts of wild places were put to the back of mind but lay dormant until a chance encounter in my local library reignited my interest.

I was in my late 20s when I discovered a book entitled *Wales* by W.A.Poucher who was the pre-eminent British mountain photographer of the 1940s, 50s and 60s. His photographs in *Wales* and in other books I later acquired alerted me to the wealth of natural splendour available to us in Great Britain. It wasn't too long before myself and a couple of friends took our first baby steps in the mountains with a trip to the Lake District where we climbed Harrison Stickle in the Langdale Pikes. After that first trip I became obsessed with the high and wild places, embarking on a journey which would see me walking, scrambling, rock climbing and winter mountaineering all over the UK. Ten years later and with a huge desire to share with others the beauty of the hills I decided that photography was the perfect medium in which to inspire others in much the same way as Mr. Poucher had inspired me. The power of mountain photography cannot be underestimated and an evocative image can profoundly influence the viewer in ways that he or she may not realise. At least that is how it was for me.

In 2013 a change in my personal circumstances presented me with the chance to start a brand-new life in Snowdonia, a life which I could dedicate to the mountains. I could get to know them intimately and photograph them in all four seasons. Forever. At the time it was a daunting prospect but I grasped the opportunity with both hands and never looked back. The rest, as they say, is history and since my move I have only left Wales on a handful of occasions when absolutely necessary.

Opposite left: Mr. Frosty.
Top right: *Tryfan in winter – 2008.*
Bottom right: *Soloing the Dolmen Ridge on Glyder Fach – 2014.* **Photo**: © *Jock Andrews.*

My story, my mountains

It is said that familiarity breeds contempt but in my experience it has enabled me to acquire a deeper understanding of the landscape, culture and moods of this magnificent area. Each time I gaze upon a Snowdonian mountain-scape and set out to compose an image, what lies before me is more than just a grand vista at which to point my camera. My reaction to a scene goes far beyond its physical configuration or how the light falls upon it and in quiet moments of reflection what I actually perceive is an unfolding story which began many years ago on my first visit to these mountains. Wherever I happen to place my tripod, every ridge, summit, lake and crag I see hold memories of days spent either alone or with friends; most are happy and some are bitter sweet but all are precious adding a rich personal narrative to my photographic work which transcends the simple act of collecting images. My most heartfelt desire is that I should be fortunate enough to enjoy many more years living and working in my beloved Snowdonia.

Eryri am byth.

On Amphitheatre Buttress – 2008.
***Opposite**: On Tryfan's Grooved Arete – 2010.*

Nick Livesey mountain images

Nick has been taking a camera with him into the mountains for almost two decades, but it was in 2010 when he really caught the landscape photography bug and he bought a decent compact camera, the Canon G12. His photography quickly became popular at the *UKClimbing.com* galleries and in 2012 he came third overall and won the *Winter Walking and Scrambling* categories in the UKC/UKH Mountain Photography Awards. That year also saw Nick commended in *Landscape Photographer of the Year* (LPOTY) with a shot taken on a £60 compact camera.

Up until his move to Wales in 2013 he regularly visited all the main upland areas of the UK on walking, climbing and photography trips but since then, he has concentrated on his home patch and has developed extensive knowledge and experience of all the Snowdonian mountain ranges, culminating in his first book, *Photographing The Snowdonia Mountains* (fotoVUE 2018).

In 2014, Nick, with John Rowell and Marion Waine, opened the Soul of *Snowdonia Gallery* hosted by the Moel Siabod Cafe in Capel Curig selling framed prints, calendars and greeting cards.

A colourful personality with a compelling back story have made Nick a sought after speaker and the subject of many interviews on various websites and magazines such as *The Great Outdoors, ON Landscape, Outdoor Photography, UKHillwalking.com* and *Summit* as well as being a regular contributor to the routes section of *TRAIL* magazine. In 2017 he was featured in the award winning and critically acclaimed film short *My Mountain Healing* by Film up High.

As a qualified mountain leader and outdoor first aider Nick offers mountain photography workshops and photo guiding throughout Snowdonia National Park.

nicklivesey.co.uk .... soulofsnowdonia.co.uk

A November afternoon above Llyn Gwynant with Moel Hebog and Yr Aran beyond. Canon 6D, 24-70mm at 24mm, ISO 100, 1/30 sec at f/11, 1.5 graduated filter, tripod.

An April evening on Castell y Gwynt ,Glyder Fach. Canon 6D, 24-70mm at 26mm, ISO 100, 0.5 sec at f/11, 0.9 graduated filter, tripod.

FotoVUE

fotoVUE publishes photo-location and travel guidebooks, to the world's most beautiful places, helping anyone with a camera to take their best photographs.

These are the books currently available. Go to our website: **fotovue.com** for a list of forthcoming titles and to subscribe to our monthly newsletter.

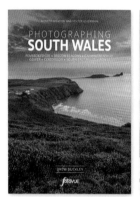
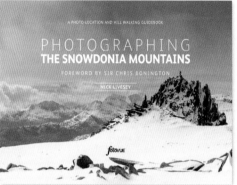
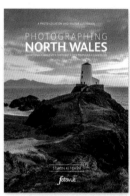

— THE WELSH COLLECTION —

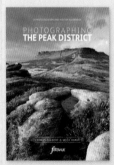
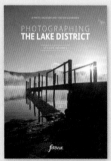

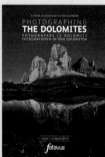

Opposite: Observing the Milky Way as it hangs above the north faces of the Trees Come Lavaredo. Nikon D810, 14-24mm at 14mm, ISO3200, 30s at f.2.8, July. Image taken from **Photographing the Dolomites** *by James Rushforth. It is the complete photo-location and travel guidebook to the Dolomites.*